ZAMBIA

Timothy Holmes & Winnie Wong

Marshall Cavendish
Benchmark

New York

PICTURE CREDITS
Cover photo: © Sean Sprague/Peter Arnold, Inc.
alt.TYPE/REUTERS: 28, 85, 112 • Andes Press Agency: 67, 79 • Bart Versteeg: 48, 73, 82, 86, 91 • Bes Stock: 7 • Capelo & Ivens (from De Angola a Contracosta, Lisbon, 1886): 101 • Corbis Inc.: 23, 30, 33, 40, 41, 47, 60, 74, 75, 122, 123, 127, 129 • Focus Team—Italy: 89 • Getty Images: 16, 31, 39, 54, 84, 102, 104 • Hulton Getty: 18, 22, 26 • Hutchison Library: 4, 66, 108 • Ian Murphy: 10, 12, 44, 46, 57, 59, 61, 63, 65, 81, 120, 121 • Images of Africa: 43, 51 • Lonely Planet Images: 1, 3, 5, 13, 56, 64, 69, 72, 78, 96, 98 • Marek Patzer: 9, 11, 15, 77, 118, 119 • National Archive, Zambia: 32 • National Geographic society Images: 52, 53, 55, 58, 80 • Norfiszuwaan Mohd Ahbar: 130, 131 • Photolibrary.com: 21, 92 • Pilcher Graphics: 35, 83, 93, 94, 97, 100, 113, 114, 116 • Serpa Pinto (from How I crossed Africa, London, 1881): 19 • Sipho Phiri: 106 • TEELO: 37, 70, 71, 76, 103, 105, 107, 109 • Toni Tilley (illustration by Stephen Kappata): 109 • TopFoto: 14, 24, 25 • William Phiri: 17

PRECEDING PAGE
Zambian children grinning for the camera.

Editorial Director (U.S.): Michelle Bisson
Editors: Deborah Grahame, Mabelle Yeo, Mindy Pang
Copyreader: Sherry Chiger
Designer: Lock Hong Liang
Cover picture researcher: Connie Gardner
Picture researcher: Thomas Khoo

Marshall Cavendish Benchmark
99 White Plains Road
Tarrytown, NY 10591
Web site: www.marshallcavendish.us

All Internet sites were correct and accurate at the time of printing. All monetary figures in this publication are in U.S. dollars.

Library of Congress Cataloging-in-Publication Data
Holmes, Timothy.
  Zambia / by Timothy Holmes & Winnie Wong. — Rev. ed.
    p. cm.
  Summary: "Provides comprehensive information on the geography, history, wildlife, governmental structure, economy, cultural diversity, peoples, religion, and culture of Zambia"--Provided by publisher.
  Includes bibliographical references and index.
  ISBN 978-0-7614-3039-1
  1. Zambia—Juvenile literature. I. Wong, Winnie. II. Title.

DT3042.H64 2009
968.94—dc22   2007050794

Printed in China

9 8 7 6 5 4 3 2 1

CONTENTS

A Kunda girl from the Kawaza village in South Luangwa carries her sibling on a slinged cloth.

A shawl secures this sleeping child as her mother works the fields.

INTRODUCTION

ZAMBIA, HOME TO THE SPECTACULAR VICTORIA FALLS, is landlocked in the south-central part of Africa. Shaped like a giant butterfly, it has an expansive highland plateau boasting of prolific wildlife around great rivers, spectacular lakes, and some of the world's finest national parks. Scottish explorer David Livingstone came to this area in the mid-19th century. Before European colonization the people governed themselves in kingdoms, chieftaincies, and village groups. The copper-mining industry propelled Zambia into the modern world. Although the country is rich in natural endowments, it suffers severe tribulations as well, including unemployment, inflation, and AIDS/HIV. All is not lost, however, as foreign aid pours in to help Zambia develop new sources of revenue and improve the life of its people.

GEOGRAPHY

ZAMBIA IS A LARGE COUNTRY sprawling across the plateau of south-central Africa. It is 290,586 square miles (752,614 square km) in extent, which makes it slightly larger than Texas. Zambia is landlocked, the coasts of the Indian and Atlantic oceans being some 600 miles (1,000 km) away. It is surrounded by Zimbabwe, Botswana, and Namibia to the south; Tanzania, Malawi, and Mozambique to the east; the Democratic Republic of Congo to the north; and Angola to the west.

The Zambian Plateau lies about 3,000 feet (966 m) above sea level. There are no real mountains, but the highest point (8,503 feet/2,592 m) is an unnamed location in the Mafinga Hills. The most distinctive features of the landscape are the deep gorges and valleys of the lower Zambezi and Luangwa rivers. Their precipitous escarpments look like mountains from below. These troughs are limbs of the Great African Rift Valley, which extends from Mozambique to the Red Sea.

LAND OF LAKES AND RIVERS

In the far north of Zambia, the Rift Valley contains Lake Tanganyika, more than 420 miles (676 km) long and averaging about 31 miles (50 km) wide. Only a small part of the lake lies in Zambia. The lake area is a place of indescribable beauty, attracting visitors from around the world.

Zambia takes its name from the magnificent river Zambezi, which rises in the northwest near the border between Congo and Angola, then travels 1,700 miles (2,736 km) to its mouth on the Indian Ocean in Mozambique. The first one-third of its journey is across a wide plain that floods at the end of the rainy season. Farther downstream, the Kariba

Above: **The Zambezi River in Zambia.**

Opposite: **Many of the waterfalls along the Zambezi River have been declared national monuments, or harnessed to generate energy.**

An elephant herd walking by the Luangwa, a river that connects to the Zambezi River.

Dam blocks the river's gorge to form the man-made Lake Kariba. Here, two hydropower stations supply electricity to Zambia and Zimbabwe. The Kafue River, likewise dammed for electricity, and then the Luangwa join the Zambezi before flowing into Mozambique. In northern Zambia the largest river is the Chambeshi. It rises near the Tanzania border, flows into Lake Bangweulu and its surrounding wetlands, and emerges with a new name, Luapula. It feeds into Lake Mweru, emerges renamed Lualaba, which downstream becomes the Congo, and flows into the Atlantic Ocean. North-flowing rivers in Zambia flow to the Atlantic and south-flowing rivers into the Indian Ocean.

There are beautiful waterfalls on all the northern rivers. The most spectacular of these is Kalambo Falls, the second highest waterfall in Africa, which plunges in a single drop of about 726 feet (221 m) over the Lake Tanganyika escarpment. Many of Zambia's waterfalls have been declared national monuments, which means that they and the environment around them are protected from human defacement. In traditional religion the waterfalls were believed to be the abode of the spirits of the ancestors, but this has not prevented some of them from being used to generate electricity.

CLIMATE

All the rivers mentioned have their origins on Zambian soil, which indicates good rainfall. The country does in fact enjoy a favorable rainfall pattern, though there have been disastrous droughts, most notably in the 1930s and the early 1990s. Approximately 10 million people in Zambia and Malawi suffered from lack of food in the drought of 2005.

The rainy season, the equivalent of the Asian monsoon, starts around the end of October and lasts until March or April. The rest of the year can be totally dry, with clear blue skies day after day. Rain is, of course, vital for agriculture but has an extra significance for Zambia, where more than 90 percent of all electricity is produced by hydropower. The droughts of the early 1990s left the water level in the Kariba and Kafue dams so low that it was hardly a few inches above the intake of the generators.

Zambia lies between 8° and 18° south of the equator and is thus a tropical land. But the elevation of the plateau above sea level gives the country a more pleasant climate than that of most other tropical lands. The temperature on the plateau rarely rises above 95°F (35°C). During the short winter, from June to August, there can even be frost on the plateau. The deep valleys, however, are much warmer, with temperatures exceeding 105°F (41°C). The hottest and most unpleasant phase is the period of six weeks or so before the onset of the rains, when people can get very uncomfortable. The first thunderstorms bring relief and refreshment.

Forests cover an extensive part of Zambia. They appear uniform from afar but contain hundreds of species of trees.

9

Above: **The baobab, sometimes called the upside-down tree because its branches look like roots, reaches a girth so large that is possible to make a dwelling in its hollow trunk.**

Opposite: **Pesticides have entered the food chain of the fish eagle around Lake Kariba, causing a great reduction in its numbers.**

Around Zambia's built-up areas, many natural forests have been cleared for timber or fuel.

VEGETATION

Most of Zambia is flat and covered by savanna woodland, open forest that varies in height and density according to rainfall and soil conditions. In the drier low-lying valleys the tree cover is much more open. Palms and enormous, fantastic baobabs are common. Where the forest is crisscrossed by drainage lines the land is suitable for agriculture, while the open plains of the Kafue and Upper Zambezi rivers provide excellent grazing for cattle.

Where the forest has been cleared for farming it is possible to clearly see the abundance and enormous size—sometimes as large as a cottage—of the "anthills" built by termites. The termitaria (nests of termites) carry their own unique vegetation and during the rainy season sprout edible mushrooms; one type of mushroom has a cap a yard (0.91 m) in diameter, making it the largest mushroom in the world.

Although in some areas trees have to be removed to make way for agriculture, industry, and human settlement, extensive areas have been set aside as forest reserves. In the national parks the natural vegetation, from the tallest trees to the smallest flowers, is as much protected as the wildlife.

ANIMAL LIFE

Zambia has a multitude of species living in their natural habitats. Nineteen national parks have been set aside to conserve different ecologies and their wildlife. For example, the Kasanka National Park, adjoining the Lake Bangweulu Swamp, is conserving two rare antelopes—the black lechwe and the shy sitatunga. The Lochinvar National Park in the south is the home of thousands of red lechwes—long-horned antelopes that have adapted to life on a floodplain—and more than 400 species of birds, especially waterfowl such as pelicans, spoonbills, and the huge Goliath heron. Other notable birds along the waterways are the African fish eagle and the Marabou stork, which nests in the cliffs of Kalambo Falls. Migrants from the northern hemisphere visit during the rainy season and bring the number of bird species recorded in Zambia to 699.

The incredibly varied fish life of Lake Tanganyika is conserved in the marine extension of the Nsumbu National Park. The lake contains around 450 identified species, many of which, having evolved in isolation, are unique to Zambia. These include hundreds of species of iridescent cichlids and two species of the sardinelike *kapenta* (kah-paint-ah), which have been successfully transplanted to Lake Kariba. The largest fish in the lake are the giant catfish (200 pounds/91 kg), the Nile perch (130 pounds/59 kg), and the Goliath tiger fish (50 pounds/23 kg).

An aerial view of Lusaka, the bustling and vibrant, colorful and cosmopolitan capital of Zambia.

Kafue National Park and Luangwa National Park abound in big game, with thousands of elephants, buffalo, and large antelopes such as sable, roan, eland, and kudu. Lions and leopards are common, too. In Luangwa, a unique species of giraffe is found. Unfortunately the black rhinoceros is extinct locally, slaughtered by poachers to satisfy the market demand for its horn in East Asia; the elephant is under constant threat for its ivory.

THE CITIES

The small capitals of the *litunga*, or king of the Lozi, on the Upper Zambezi, and the *mwata kazembe*, or king of the Lunda, on the Luapula River, give an idea of what a precolonial Zambian town was like.

Unlike other African countries such as Ethiopia and Zimbabwe, Zambia does not have ancient cities, either standing or in ruins. Most Zambians were seminomadic, their rulers shifting the government base from place to place at frequent intervals.

The country's current urban centers were all built during the past century. Their architecture and street plans are Western in style, and

The modern buildings found in the mining and business city of Kitwe along the Copperbelt.

until shortly before Zambia's independence they were segregated along racial lines. In the Copperbelt, the towns started as mining camps, each close to a copper-ore body. Kabwe, in Central Province, was built adjacent to the old Broken Hill lead and zinc mine. Ndola and Kitwe, the largest cities in the Copperbelt, each have a population of about 1.6 million people, while Kabwe has about 250,000. They are all busy industrial and commercial centers, with the Copperbelt consuming more than 75 percent of the electricity used in Zambia.

Livingstone, Zambia's first capital, and Lusaka, the current seat of government, have different origins from the mining centers.

LUSAKA—FROM RAILWAY SIDING TO MODERN CAPITAL

In the early years of the 20th century, Lusaka started its existence as a railway siding, a section of railway track used to allow trains on the same tracks to pass one another. It was named after the local chief, a famous

Though the cities and towns have expanded, the population far exceeds the numbers the cities were planned for. Only a few residents have access to all the amenities of developed urban life.

Stanley House and the Capitol in Livingstone. Like many other buildings in Zambia's cities, these were built during the colonial period.

elephant hunter, and grew to be the commercial center for white farmers in the district. In 1935, because of its central position in the territory, the British colonial government made Lusaka the capital of what was then known as Northern Rhodesia and developed it on the pattern of an English "garden city." Buildings including the State House, the High Court, and the Secretariat were erected at this time, followed by the impressive Anglican Cathedral. After independence in 1964, the imposing National Assembly, with its copper roof; the University of Zambia; the International Airport terminal; and many more state and commercial buildings joined the skyline.

Lusaka was planned for 200,000 residents, but today it has a population exceeding 1 million, living mostly in poor conditions. From its beginnings as a small outpost of the British Empire, it has transformed itself into the hub of Zambia and of Central Africa, with highway, air, and rail links.

LIVINGSTONE—COLONIAL AND PREHISTORIC HERITAGE

The city of Livingstone, built as a commercial center on high ground overlooking Victoria Falls, was established when the railway from South Africa crossed the Zambezi on the bridge just below the falls in 1904. The town was made the capital of Northern Rhodesia in 1911. It takes its name from the Scottish explorer and missionary Dr. David Livingstone, who in 1855 saw the great waterfall for the first time and named it after the reigning queen of England, Victoria. The name is used in Zambia alongside its original name—Mosi-O-Tunya, or "The Smoke That Thunders."

In 1935 Lusaka replaced Livingstone as capital, but the latter remains a place of great historical interest, apart from being beside the falls. Zambia's national museum, the Livingstone Museum, and an open archaeological site, the Field Museum, which is next to the falls, show the development of Homo sapiens in the area from the early Stone Age to the present, spanning more than 250,000 years of human history.

The early colonial buildings of the town give a glimpse of the more recent past, while the Railway Museum holds a fine collection of locomotives and rolling stock from the age of steam. For these and other reasons, not least Victoria Falls, Livingstone is known as the Tourist Capital of Zambia.

HISTORY

ZAMBIA'S FRONTIERS WERE DRAWN on the map of Africa about a century ago by European imperial powers, and it is thus a relatively new country. Humans and their predecessors have inhabited it for a quarter of a million years, however, as archaeological records show. The skull of Broken Hill Man (now in the British Museum, London), found near the Kabwe lead and zinc mine in 1921, is that of a Neanderthal, a type of people who made stone tools and lived by hunting and gathering.

Bola Stone

THE STONE AGE

About 15,000 years ago, during the late Stone Age, people evolved into modern humans, making sophisticated tools and decorating their rock shelters with pictures. These are the ancestors of the present-day San, or Bushmen, of southern Africa, a few of whom are still found in Zambia. They were of small stature and lived in family groups, following the herds of migratory antelopes they hunted. They also ate tubers, wild fruit, and honey gathered from the wild but did not grow crops, keep livestock, or construct dwellings. Skeletons found at one of their sites beside a hot spring in southern Zambia indicate that they suffered from tooth decay.

One of their hunting weapons was similar to the South American bola—stone spheres tied to the ends of a rope that when thrown brought an antelope down by entangling its legs. These people are thought to have held the eland, the largest of African antelopes, as sacred; a surviving Zambian rock painting depicts the animal. The San lived in Zambia for thousands of years but were eventually superseded by a people who started arriving more than 1,600 years ago.

17

When Europeans arrived in the 19th century, Zambia was populated by the Bemba, the Lunda, the Chewa, the Lozi, and the Ngoni, among other people.

The smelting of iron or copper was regarded as a mystic act. Copper cast in the form of a cross was used as currency.

IRON AGE IMMIGRANTS

About the fourth century A.D., people who made and used iron, kept livestock, grew crops, and lived in houses began to occupy Zambia from the north. They formed part of the slow migration of tall, dark-skinned people originating, it is believed, in the east of modern Nigeria. Over a period of more than a thousand years they took over nearly all of Africa south of latitude 5° north. In parts of Zambia these people displaced the San; in other parts both lived side by side. The immigrants, known as the Bantu, were mining and smelting iron and copper 1,500 years ago and making weapons, fishhooks, and household items with the metals. They also baked clay pots and beakers. About A.D.1000, further Bantu immigration led to a consequent admixture that gave rise to the ancestors of the present-day Zambian people.

Meanwhile, in what is today southern Congo, to the north of Zambia, two Bantu groups, the Lunda and the Luba, were developing into kingdoms.

Between A.D. 1500 and 1750, offshoots from these kingdoms moved into Zambia. They conquered all but the southern part of the territory and formed kingdoms of their own. Previously Zambians had lived in small self-governing societies without a central political authority.

THE KINGDOMS

For a while some kingdoms in Zambia were ruled by the Lunda emperor, the *mwata yamvo*, but in time they all became self-governing. In the north were the Bemba, ruled by the *chitimukulu*, or chieftain; in the Luapula Valley, a breakaway Lunda tribe was ruled by the *mwata kazembe*; in the east were the Maravi, ancestors of today's Chewa; and in the west, on the Upper Zambezi, were the Lozi, who were ruled by a *litunga*. Each king made subjects of the surrounding inhabitants so that his nominal territory was extensive and held together by patronage and tribute.

Lubosi, later called Lewanika the First, was a precolonial king of the Lozi people. The Lozi were defeated by the Makololo in the first half of the 19th century. Three decades later, they defeated the Makololo and restored their kingdom.

In the first half of the 19th century, two new groups of conquerors arrived from what is now the Republic of South Africa. A host of Ngoni, led by Zwangendaba, and another of Makololo, who were led by Sebitwane, entered eastern and western Zambia respectively across the Zambezi. The Ngoni, who spoke Zulu, established a kingdom under Mpezeni I among the conquered Chewa.

The Makololo defeated and took over the Lozi kingdom. The Ngoni tried repeatedly to conquer the Bemba, without success, but secured their

*Zambia saw an
influx of Western
traders, explorers,
and missionaries
during the 19th
century.*

place permanently in eastern Zambia. The Makololo survived for only three decades. Weakened by malaria, to which they had no immunity, they were easily overthrown by the Lozi they had once subjected.

THE OUTSIDE WORLD MOVES IN

The first contact between different peoples is often the result of trade. From the earliest times in the Zambian area of the African interior, there had been exchanges of goods between producers of different commodities—for instance, between salt miners and metal workers or between fishermen and makers of cloth. Some of this trading, especially if it dealt with valuables such as copper and ivory, reached the coast.

The eastern seaboard of Africa had, from the days of ancient Egypt, been part of a trading network that extended to South and Southeast Asia and later to China. In the time of the Zambian kingdoms, this trade was in the hands of the Swahili, Muslim African-Arabs living in city-states along the coast and on nearby islands. By A.D. 1400, people in Zambia on the Zambezi near Kariba were importing jewelry from Asia.

On the Atlantic coast, the Portuguese established trading ports in the 16th century. By 1850 their merchants had reached central Zambia. The Portuguese were also in Mozambique, having driven out the Swahili, with a trading town as far up the Zambezi as where it is joined by the Luangwa River. The Swahili of Zanzibar, too, were penetrating the interior, and by the mid-19th century one of their merchants had crossed Africa from the Indian Ocean to the Atlantic.

Zambia thus became involved with both the Portuguese and the Swahili mercantile empires. Money was hardly used for trade. What the Zambian rulers wanted most were colored and patterned cloth, jewelry, firearms, and distilled alcohol such as rum and cane spirit.

In exchange, they bartered local products such as beeswax, iron, copper, and the more valuable ivory, rhinoceros horns, and slaves.

From the west coast, the Portuguese shipped the slaves to mines and sugar plantations in Brazil. Slaves taken to the east coast could find themselves as far from home as the Middle East, India, and China. Many millions of Africans suffered this fate. Domestic slavery was an accepted part of the Zambian social order, and many kings took part in its natural extension, the slave trade, which was not suppressed until the end of the 19th century.

CHRISTIAN MISSIONARIES

Slavery was abolished in the British Empire during the 1830s, partly as a result of the moral crusade waged by Christian abolitionists such as William Wilberforce. One of his followers, a Scottish medical missionary named David Livingstone, started working in southern Africa in 1840. During a visit to King Sebitwane of the Makololo on the Zambezi in 1851, Livingstone saw the slave trade in operation and decided to help put an end to it. His plan was to establish settlements where slaves who were being exported would instead work at home and produce crops, particularly cotton, for sale in Britain.

Livingstone died in Zambia in 1863, without success in his venture, but his life and ideas inspired other missionaries. Two of the earliest of these were François Coillard, a French Protestant who opened a mission

David Livingstone.

David Livingstone's motto was "Christianity, Commerce, and Civilization," and he was influenced in his thinking by the achievements of Sir Thomas Stamford Raffles and Sir James Brook, raja of Sarawak.

21

Cecil Rhodes (1853–1902) helped to bring the territory—under the name Northern Rhodesia—into the British Empire by the end of the 19th century.

to the Lozi of the Upper Zambezi in 1884, and Henri Dupont, a French Catholic priest who did likewise among the Bemba in the north during the 1890s. They were followed by others, Protestant and Roman Catholic.

Meanwhile, believing that Zambia was rich in gold, the British South African mining magnate and avowed imperialist Cecil John Rhodes was seeking ways to colonize the region.

COLONIAL RULE

From the 1890s until 1923 the area that is now Zambia was administered by Rhodes's British South Africa Company (BSAC) under a concession granted by Queen Victoria. Coillard had persuaded the Lozi *litunga*, Lewanika, to sign a treaty with the BSAC, and Dupont engineered the submission of the Bemba. Other kings—the *mpezeni* of the Ngoni and the *mwata kazembe* of the Luapula Lunda—were overcome by force of arms. Soon the whole territory was under BSAC control and the current boundaries largely drawn.

Rhodes's dream of Zambian gold did not materialize, but large tracts of land were taken over by white settlers. Although the BSAC abolished slavery, Zambians were subjected to a system of forced labor intended to supply manpower for the gold and diamond mines of South Africa. It was a new form of servitude. Direct British rule after the departure of the

BSAC in 1923 was more benign, though the white settlers were highly privileged, and racial discrimination became the law of the land.

During the 1920s the rich ore bodies deep underground along the Copperbelt began to be exploited. Skilled white miners were brought in from South Africa and Britain, while the large, unskilled workforce needed for mining was drawn from all corners of Zambia. The Copperbelt became a melting pot in which a Zambian national identity was born out of the many groups that lived within the country's frontiers.

The discovery of copper along the Copperbelt led to an influx of migrants, who were brought in to work in the mines.

A long line of women voters outside a polling station in Lusaka during the first general election for Northern Rhodesia, on January 22, 1964.

By the end of World War II, in which Zambian troops served with distinction in Burma, Zambia had become one of the world's top producers of refined copper. But Zambian workers in the mines suffered racial discrimination—the "color bar" that kept them in unskilled positions.

A trade-union movement developed, while on the political front the voice of Zambian nationalism demanding an end to colonial rule was heard ever more loudly. Lawrence Katilungu headed the Mine Workers Union, while the nationalist leader was Harry Mwaanga Nkumbula, with his African National Congress (ANC) behind him.

FEDERATION

Another postwar development was the plan by the white settlers in Northern and Southern Rhodesia to consolidate their power by federating the two territories. Despite widespread opposition in Zambia, including by some whites, federation was imposed in 1953. The Federation of Rhodesia and Nyasaland, consisting of the territories of Northern and Southern Rhodesia and Nyasaland (present-day Malawi), was dominated by white supremacists and was a major obstacle to the establishment of independence for Zambia.

The Zambians' struggle against white supremacy and colonial rule thus gathered momentum. Nkumbula and his ANC seemed unequal to the task,

Northern Rhodesia's pre-independence all-black cabinet after being sworn in, with the governor of Northern Rhodesia, Sir Evelyn Hone (*front, third from left*), and deputy governor F. M. Thomas. Kenneth Kaunda stands next to the governor, and Simon Kapwepwe stands at the back.

President Kaunda at the Commonwealth Conference on June 8, 1977, with British prime minister James Callaghan.

and a new liberation movement, the United National Independence Party (UNIP, pronounced "yoo-neep"), was formed in 1958. Its most energetic figures were Kenneth David Kaunda and Simon Mwansa Kapwepwe.

So effective was UNIP's campaigning that the federation collapsed in 1963. Nyasaland became independent as Malawi a year later, in July 1964. Zambia became an independent republic on October 24, 1964, installing Kaunda as president. The British government retained Southern Rhodesia as a colony until 1980, when white minority domination gave way to majority rule and the country was named Zimbabwe.

INDEPENDENCE

Zambia entered independence with sails full of wind. Copper prices were high, and the economy was in good shape, promising the resources to correct the inequalities of the colonial past. Schools, colleges, and a university were built and health services greatly improved. Free universal primary schooling was implemented, secondary school enrollment quadrupled, and adult illiteracy was tackled. Plans were drawn up to transform Zambia into a modern, industrialized state with the economy run by Zambians, not foreign-owned mining houses. It was anticipated that agriculture would outstrip copper as the principal earner of hard currency.

In November 1965 the dominant white population of Southern Rhodesia declared unilateral independence from Britain, and Zambia was drawn into what would become the Southern Rhodesian liberation war.

Apart from the material damage Zambia suffered, its plans for economic development were thrown out of joint. In addition to the conflict between the black and white communities in Southern Rhodesia, Zambia was affected by the wars against the Portuguese colonialists in Mozambique and Angola, the struggle against apartheid in South Africa, and the war against South African occupation in Namibia. These events served only to distract the Zambian government from domestic priorities and to lead to the diversion of resources to unproductive expenditures.

By 1975 the Portuguese had withdrawn from Africa, and the Mozambique peace treaty was signed in Lusaka. But the war in what was to become Zimbabwe continued until 1980 and that in Namibia lasted until Namibia won independence in 1990. South Africa, meanwhile, was not freed from apartheid until 1994.

THE ONE-PARTY STATE

When President Kaunda introduced a one-party state in 1972, it was not, as one might suppose, as a government of national unity in the face of the wars underway among Zambia's neighbors. It was a move to accord supremacy to UNIP and to allow Kaunda to maintain his presidency by promoting unity and economic development.

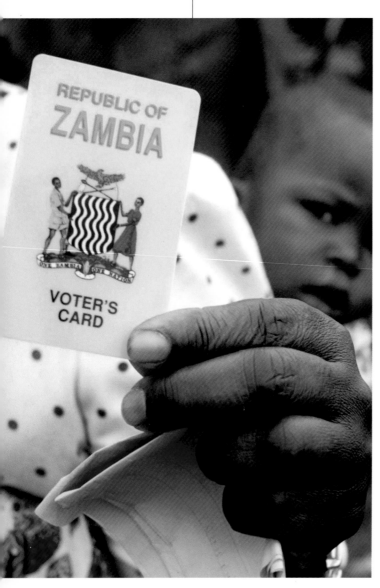

Kaunda nationalized 80 percent of the economy, including the mining industry. The civil service, police, and defense forces were politicized, and an all-pervasive secret police force was created. Opponents were jailed, often for years without trial, with many tortured and some murdered. The president, who called his ideology Zambian Humanism, became a dictator. Though officially a "participatory democracy," the one-party state was authoritarian. Corruption, inefficiency, maladministration, and nepotism ruined the economy and perverted civil society.

The country was saved from collapse only when Kaunda was persuaded, partly by the donors upon whom the economy was by then dependent, to restore democracy. Apart from an abortive military coup in which no one was hurt, and sporadic rioting in which about 20 people were gunned down, no widespread violence occurred before Kaunda agreed to multiparty voting.

Free elections were held in October 1991. Kaunda and his party, UNIP, were voted out of office by a wide margin. Former union leader Frederick Chiluba,

Opposite: **A woman holds up a voting card used for elections.**

who headed the Movement for Multiparty Democracy (MMD), succeeded Kaunda as president.

The constitution of Zambia was subsequently amended in 1996, with the introduction by Chiluba's government of a controversial provision that allowed only candidates whose families had been established in Zambia for at least two generations to run for presidency. This automatically disqualified Kaunda, whose parents were from Malawi. Presidents were also not to serve more than two terms in office under this new constitution. With these changes, Chiluba was elected to his second term as president in the November 1996 elections. In 2001 efforts by Chiluba's supporters to push for yet another amendment to the constitution, to provide for a third term of office for Chiluba, failed, and Levy Mwanawasa, a presidential candidate of the MMD, defeated all opposition candidates to succeed Chiluba as president in 2002.

Far from being a puppet of his predecessor, Mwanawasa began his term determined to fight corruption and spearhead intense efforts to reduce Zambia's foreign debt and increase economic growth. Huge economic challenges awaited the new president. In 2003 Chiluba was arrested, and many charges of corruption have since been brought against him. The High Court in Britain ruled in 2007 that Chiluba and his aides had been involved in stealing a whopping $46 million from Zambia. In 2005, due to Mwanawasa's dedication to solving Zambia's economic woes, the World Bank approved a debt-relief package that wrote off more than half of the country's external debt. Substantial progress in privatization and signs of economic recovery began to take form with a series of budgetary reforms and the continued fight against the ravages of corruption. In September 2006 Mwanawasa, respected for his integrity, was reelected to serve his second term as leader of Zambia.

GOVERNMENT

WHEN ZAMBIA BECAME AN INDEPENDENT REPUBLIC in October 1964, there were only a few trained and educated Zambians capable of running the government. The economy was largely dependent on foreign expertise.

The later transition from one-party rule to a democratic government was both troubling and exhilarating. It was disruptive because Zambians have for ages been accustomed to authoritarian rule. The precolonial kings and chiefs were hardly democrats; neither were the British governors nor the one-party president. It was exhilarating because people could now do things that had been out of the question before, such as debating hot issues in public, staging antigovernment demonstrations, and taking a cabinet minister to court.

The Zambian experience has shown that an entrenched one-party dictatorship cannot be reformed; it has to be uprooted and replaced by new structures.

Left: **The leader of Zambia's opposition, Michael Sata, protests against proposed tax reforms that could leave the poor in a worse plight than before.**

Opposite: **The Non-Aligned Summit Monument in Lusaka.**

Harry Nkumbula is one of several political leaders in Zambia who started their career in the labor movement.

Dismantling the apparatus of the one-party state has been painful for some. To bolster its support, the previous government had created innumerable unproductive jobs in the civil service and state-owned enterprises for its supporters. Such employment ceased when the civil service was trimmed to an efficient size, and state companies, most notably Zambia Airways, have closed down or been sold to private investors who run them as real businesses. There is a close connection in Zambia between politics and the government's economic policies, and every move is scrutinized. The public pounces on any sign of reversion to dictatorial ways by the president, ministers, or state officials. People expect perfection, but there may be many disappointments, as democracy does not come ready-made like a mass-produced automobile.

MAKING THE CONSTITUTION

Zambia is a republic with a presidential system of government, like that of France and the United States and unlike the systems in India and Germany, where the head of state is nonexecutive. Since independence in 1964 Zambia has had three constitutions, the current state being known as the Third Republic.

The independence constitution negotiated by Zambia's nationalists and the colonial powers was enacted by the British parliament. It provided for universal adult suffrage, a directly elected executive president, and a national assembly from whose members the president would appoint a cabinet. Freedom of association was enshrined, which meant that anyone could form a political party.

The first president was Kenneth Kaunda. His United National Independence Party (UNIP) had a majority in the Zambian parliament, with Harry Nkumbula's African National Congress (ANC) and a party representing mainly whites in opposition.

For a few years Zambia enjoyed a multiparty democracy, but UNIP had always been intent on a one-party state, following Lenin in Russia and Kwame Nkrumah, the first president of Ghana and an influential figure in Africa's emancipation from colonialism. Kaunda appointed a constitutional-review commission, which toured the country to assess opinion and duly issued a report that broadly favored UNIP's plans. Kaunda, however, rejected its recommendation that a president should serve only two terms in office. After UNIP came to an agreement with Nkumbula on sharing the spoils of office, ANC ceased to exist, and the "one-party participatory democracy" was ushered in with Kaunda as president and a few ex-ANC members of parliament—but not Nkumbula—in the cabinet.

Under the constitution of the Second Republic, UNIP was the only party allowed. State and party were amalgamated, with the party supreme and the cabinet subordinate to UNIP's central committee. Parliament became a rubber stamp, and members who expressed criticism or asked awkward questions were removed. A state of emergency was permanently in force, so that citizens could enjoy only such rights as the president conceded. Radio, television, the press, and publishing were placed under state control.

Orphans eat lunch at the Motaru Catholic Church. According to the constitution of the Third Republic, orphans who cannot prove their parentage are ineligible to be president.

The constitution is now law, but public debate on issues continues. The constitution-making process is by no means complete.

By 1990 opposition to UNIP had become too widespread to suppress, and Kaunda reluctantly agreed to a new constitution negotiated with the recently formed Movement for Multiparty Democracy (MMD), which had the support of the Zambia Congress of Trade Unions. Civil liberties were restored, and the Third Republic was born, with Frederick Chiluba and the MMD winning the elections. The MMD had promised to review the constitution once again and appointed a commission, which included nominees of the opposition, to do so. The government accepted many of the commission's recommendations and presented these to parliament as amendments to the constitution. Parliament approved with a majority of more than two-thirds, but many people were unhappy that the matter had not been put to a referendum.

This third constitution contains a strong bill of rights similar to that of the United States and entrenches the independence of the judiciary. The president may serve only two five-year terms. But it contains two provisions that are contentious. One is its declaration of Zambia as a Christian nation. Many people, including some prominent Christians, would have preferred Zambia to be a secular state, with a clear separation between religion and politics. The second is the clause stating that only Zambian citizens whose parents are or were citizens of Zambia may become president. First-generation citizens and those who cannot prove their parentage are thus unable to aspire to the highest office in the land. A large proportion of the population is affected by this clause.

A draft constitution submitted by a commission in 2005 was rejected by Levy Mwanawasa, who had been elected president in 2002, while churches and civic and opposition groups supported the changes. Foremost among them is the requirement that a candidate receive more than 50 percent of the vote to be elected president. A new draft that still

contained that requirement and other recommendations was submitted before the end of the year, but Mwanawasa said that it could not be adopted before the 2006 presidential election. In the September 2006 presidential vote Mwanawasa won reelection with 42 percent of the vote after trailing early in the campaign.

HUMAN RIGHTS BALANCE SHEET

The constitution of Zambia guarantees freedom of expression and assembly, gives all citizens equal rights before the law, forbids ethnic and religious discrimination, and states that no person can be kept in custody for more than 48 hours before being brought before a court of law. In some areas, however, these guarantees have not been honored. For example, Zambia's main newspapers and national broadcasting corporation remain under state control. Editors and journalists who displease the government have

Like nearly all other governments, that of Zambia tends at times to exceed its constitutional powers and trample on civil liberties.

Most notable among nonpolitical groups are the trade unions and the churches. The voices of many professional bodies are authoritative: The government listens to them, even if it does not agree.

been dismissed. Moreover, the president is empowered under legislation dating from the colonial period to ban any publication he dislikes, and the laws on obscenity have very wide scope. The Public Order Act, which demands police permits for public gatherings, restricts the freedom of assembly.

In what are defined as "serious" criminal cases—for instance, murder or drug trafficking—the accused might not be granted bail, which is a detraction from the independence of the judiciary. The "citizenship" clause in the constitution concerning the presidency is seen by many as containing the seeds of ethnic discrimination. However, there have been few gross abuses of human rights since the end of the one-party state. There are no political prisoners, and the president may sustain a state of emergency without the consent of parliament only for seven days. A permanent, independent Human Rights Commission has been established, and the Police Complaints Commission is in place as well. Zambian citizens are by and large as free as those of any well-established democracy and do not hesitate to go to court if they believe their rights are being infringed upon by the state.

POLITICAL PARTIES

Zambia is a one-party dominant state, with the MMD in power. Opposition parties do have some significant representation in government. Some nine parties were listed in the September 2006 parliamentary election. The MMD took 72 seats, followed by the Patriotic Front (44 seats) and the United Democratic Alliance (27 seats), out of a total of 158 seats. The MMD enjoys nationwide support and has a strong business element in its membership and a solid following in the Copperbelt.

NATIONAL WOMEN'S LOBBY GROUP
A Government without women is like a pot sitting on one stone

VOTE FOR WOMEN

CIVIC ORGANIZATIONS

Zambians take a great interest in politics. It is often referred to as the second national sport, after soccer, but the country also has many nonpolitical civic organizations.

During election periods, independent monitoring groups come to the fore, while several societies are engaged constantly in civic education and campaigns to promote awareness of civil rights and women's interests. Journalists have set up groups to protect and extend freedom of expression. Humanitarian organizations such as the Red Cross operate freely, while among businesspeople international clubs such as the Rotary Club and the Lions are popular and involved in charitable work. Chambers of Commerce and Industry, the National Farmers' Union, the Law Association, the Economics Association of Zambia, and other professional bodies comment regularly on the performance of the government.

INTERNATIONAL RELATIONS

Zambia is at peace with its neighbors and on friendly terms with all member states of the United Nations except Iraq and Iran, with which the MMD government broke diplomatic relations because of their alleged interference in Zambian affairs.

The economy cannot sustain the cost of worldwide diplomatic representation, but Zambia has ambassadors at the UN and in major world capitals including Tokyo, Washington, London, Brussels, New Delhi, Bonn, Moscow, and Beijing. On its home continent, Zambia is represented in neighboring countries and in Kenya, Ethiopia, North Africa, and West Africa. It has established diplomatic relations worldwide with many other countries as well. Zambia is an active member of the UN, the Commonwealth of Nations, and the Organization of African Unity. On the economic front, it is a member of the Common Market for East and Southern Africa and the Southern African Development Conference. At both fronts the aim is to pursue regional cooperation. For decades Zambia, with

Opposite: **Armed policemen on patrol along the streets of Zambia.**

LOCAL GOVERNMENT

Zambia is divided into nine provinces, each with an administrative structure headed by a deputy minister appointed from parliament by the president. The country is further subdivided into 72 districts, each governed to a limited extent by elected councils responsible for such services as roads, water, health and hygiene, markets, and trading licenses. The councils, headed in the cities by an elected mayor and elsewhere by a chairperson, are supposed to finance themselves with revenue from licenses and rates. Very few are able to do so, however, so they rely on support from the central government. This is a grave weakness in the democratic structure.

the help of the UN and other agencies, has provided a safe haven for refugees from strife in Congo, Angola, Mozambique, South Africa, Namibia, Zimbabwe, and more recently, Rwanda.

DEFENSE AND SECURITY

Zambia has a small army and air force but has never been to war except indirectly, as when the country was attacked by Southern Rhodesian and South African forces during the liberation struggle against white rule in those countries. In the 1970s and 1980s the Zambian government allowed African nationalist fighters from those countries to use Zambia as a base. Since then, Zambian troops have served with UN peacekeeping units in Rwanda, Angola, and Mozambique, but at home the defense forces are engaged largely in civil operations and are politically neutral. The Staff College in Lusaka has achieved distinction and accepts military officers from neighboring countries for training. There is no conscription, and the armed forces are a professional body that accepts women as well as men.

POLICE AND COMMUNITY

The Zambia police, which was politicized under the one-party state, has been reorganized since 1991 for its role in a democracy and renamed the Zambia Police Service, with emphasis on community policing. Women often achieve senior rank. In many areas the public has formed neighborhood watches, which provide logistical support to the police, a system that has helped control crime, especially robbery and automobile theft.

ECONOMY

ZAMBIA IS AMONG THE 50 POOREST COUNTRIES in the world, though it possesses a wealth of resources. About 86 percent of the Zambian population lives below the World Bank poverty threshold of one dollar a day.

Once a middle-income country, Zambia began to slide into poverty in the 1970s, when copper prices declined on world markets. The socialist government made up for falling revenue by increasing borrowing. When the MMD took over in 1991, it found, in addition to the foreign debt, an empty treasury, a rapidly depreciating currency, and a soaring annual inflation rate. Much of the borrowed money was spent on consumption, such as food subsidies, rather than on investment. To make matters worse, nationalized industries such as the mines were mismanaged.

Zambia lies on one of the world's great mineral belts, stretching from Congo in the north to the gold mines of South Africa.

Left: **Large quarry trucks used in the copper mines of Zambia.**

Opposite: **Sheets of steel being manufactured at a factory in Zambia.**

41

ECONOMY

Despite reforms, the economy will need support from international agencies for many years to come.

Under the guidance of the World Bank and the International Monetary Fund, the new government began to implement a structural adjustment program (SAP). Its main objectives were to control inflation and stabilize the currency by cutting government expenditure to the bone. The "cash budget" principle was introduced, with the government spending no more than what it collected in revenue. All subsidies were removed, fees were brought in for social services such as education and medical attention, a value-added tax was imposed on goods and services, and, autonomous Revenue Authority was established to collect taxes and customs and excise dues. The foreign exchange market was liberalized so that the currency, the kwacha, became convertible and could be traded at market value. Its rate against the U.S. dollar has fallen from 500 kwacha in 1991 to 3,601.5 in 2007. Another SAP imperative was to replace the state-controlled economy with a market economy. By 2005, Zambians had bought about 60 percent of government-owned companies.

Increasing privatization and the implementation of a series of budgetary and structural reforms since President Mwanawasa's term of office began have served the country well. The MMD administration has been committed in its pursuit of sustainable economic growth for the country. Though Zambia is still beset by poverty, it has seen commendable improvements in its gross domestic product (GDP) and the reduction of its external debt. The confidence of investors has lifted a little with the new administration's fight against widespread corruption. Annual per capita income rose to $1,400 by 2007, with real GDP registering at $15.93 billion at a growth rate of 5.3 percent and an inflation rate of 10.5 percent that same year. The opening of new copper mines has increased copper output, and a healthy corn harvest plus continued cooperation with the international community have helped to provide an impetus to Zambia's economy.

It remains to be seen if more can be done to thoroughly rein in or remove the scourge of poverty and public debt and to put in place provisions to tackle or buffer economic shocks and shortages brought on by natural and man-made disasters.

ENERGY

Further development of Zambian mining and other industries depends on the availability of abundant, cheap electricity, most of which is produced by waterpower, which does not add to pollution. The major hydroelectric plants in Zambia are Kafue Gorge, Kariba North Bank, and Victoria Falls. There are smaller but economically important hydrostations

Power stations are on both the Zambian and Zimbabwean sides of the Kariba Dam.

Zambia has been a mining country for nearly 2,000 years and an exporter of refined copper to Asia, the Middle East, and Europe for at least 400 years.

in central Zambia, near Kabwe, at Victoria Falls, and in the north, one of which, near the Kundalila Falls, supplies the entire Eastern Province. Zambia has the capacity to export electricity to Zimbabwe, Botswana, Namibia, and South Africa. It is connected to the Congo power system, from which it imports electricity when drought affects domestic production. Petroleum products are imported from South Africa, France, and Russia. Crude oil is delivered by pipeline from the port at Dar es Salaam in Tanzania to the refinery at Ndola.

MINING

Iron and copper have been mined in Zambia for close to 2,000 years, and the country as we know it today was defined by mining. Copper, smelted and cast into bars and crosses weighing up to 50 pounds (23 kg), was an important item of trade five centuries ago. Most of the existing copper mines in the country are on the sites of ancient surface workings.

The modern mining industry reached its peak in the early 1970s, when Zambia was among the world's top four producers of refined metal and the second greatest producer of cobalt, which occurs in some of the copper-ore bodies.

Today the mining industry's copper output is about half of what it was at its peak of around 700,000 tons in the late 1970s. This is not due to a shortage of the ore but a result of the mismanagement the industry suffered during the 25 years it was under state control. The industry is now privatized, and after a low of 228,000 tons in 1998, production recovered to 337,000 tons in 2007.

Copper and cobalt have long been among Zambia's prime metals, followed by lead, zinc, gold, and manganese. A large deposit of nickel awaits exploitation, and uranium, a small amount of which was once mined in the Copperbelt, can be found in several places throughout the country. There are also large deposits of iron ore, but it has not been economically viable to develop them. Mining is not restricted to metals. There are significant reserves of gems—in particular world-class emeralds, tourmalines, aquamarines, and amethysts. Coal is also mined, as are industrial minerals such as talc, marble, limestone, and glass sand.

AGRICULTURE

Only 22 million acres out of Zambia's 148 million acres of arable land are under cultivation. Instead of being an importer, the country has the potential to be an important exporter of grain. Climate and soils make large areas of the country suitable for crops such as corn, sorghum, soybeans, rice, groundnuts, cotton, and tobacco. Wheat, coffee, and tea do well under irrigation during the long dry season. Irrigation is the basis of Zambia's most successful large-scale agricultural enterprise, the Nakambala

About 70 percent of Zambia's staple food grains are produced on small farms, where women do much of the work. Their reward is minimal, which is why many migrate to urban areas.

A worker burns off the leaves of sugarcane before the harvest.

sugar estate, owned by the privatized Zambia Sugar Company. It meets the demand within the country and exports to countries such as those of the European Union and the United States. Other export crops, most of which are sold in Europe, are cotton, tobacco, and on a small scale, vegetables, flowers, paprika, and coffee.

One of the fastest growing export industries is floriculture. The production of roses accounts for 95 percent of the industry. The Zambian floriculture industry exports 9,928 tons of fresh produce a year and contributes some $68.5 million annually to the national economy.

Cattle farming is of prime importance in regions free of the tsetse fly, which carries a deadly parasite. The fly is not common in the plateau areas of southern and eastern Zambia or on the Upper Zambezi Plains. From time immemorial cattle have been of great importance in the lives of the people there. Today commercial ranches are also large producers of beef, some of which is exported. Dairy farms, located mainly near urban centers, produce an adequate supply of fresh milk, which by law must be pasteurized before sale. There is a growing number of butter, cheese, and yogurt makers. Farmers also supply the cities but not necessarily the smaller provincial towns with chickens, eggs, pork, and fresh fruit and vegetables in abundance. But most farmers remain poor, and agriculture, particularly grain production, is not a success story.

MANUFACTURING

The liberalization of the economy since the early 1990s has had a negative effect on many Zambian industries that had been protected from imports. Competition has affected manufacturers of textiles and clothing particularly harshly. A number of state-owned enterprises such as motor assembly, industrial and domestic ceramics, and dry-cell batteries have simply collapsed.

Nonetheless, the industrial economy, which had dictated prices and is now free of state control, is in a position to flourish provided it updates its equipment, meets international standards of quality, and keeps its costs down. The domestic market is small, so for many companies the way to success will be through exports. Zambia is an active member of two economic cooperation groups spanning eastern, central, and southern Africa—the Southern Africa Development Community (SADC) and the Common Market for Eastern and Southern Africa (COMESA)—and is interested in initiating a free-trade agreement that will expand the market for Zambian products. Among industries that have established export markets are cement, refined sugar, glass, copper wire and cable, and mining explosives and equipment. New export products include jewelry, bottled lager, frozen chicken, and cheese.

A man working in a food factory in Zambia.

Zambia's highway network is centered on Lusaka, with freight and passenger services to all provinces.

The government passed the Investment Act, which gives generous incentives and tax breaks to industrialists. With Zambia's resources of electricity, metals, minerals, timber, and agricultural produce (cotton, for example), manufacturing can become a growth area of the economy, especially when foreign trade barriers are lifted.

TRANSPORTATION AND COMMUNICATION

Landlocked Zambia has two operating rail links to the sea. Zambia Railways connects the country to ports in Mozambique and South Africa, while the Tanzania Zambia Railways Authority carries freight and passengers from Kapiri Mposi to Dar es Salaam.

International road transportation has become a booming business since South Africa came out of isolation with the end of apartheid. Much of its trade with central African countries passes through Zambia. In the 1970s Zambia had one of the best highway networks in sub-Saharan Africa. Within 20 years, however, 80 percent of the road network had deteriorated. The government introduced a road fund levy on fuel, and that together with international aid has improved the highway network. In 2004 the Ministry of Works and Supply's National Road Fund Agency rated half of Zambia's paved roads in good condition and close to a quarter in fair condition.

In 1992 the state owned Zambia Airways Corporation was declared bankrupt and liquidated. Privately owned carriers, some of which also fly to neighboring countries, replaced its services on internal routes. Privately owned Zambian Airways and a number of air charter companies serve the tourism and mining industries and the government and aid sectors. Long-haul flights from Lusaka International Airport are provided by South African Airways, British Airways, Air France, and KLM Royal Dutch Airlines, among others. Main airports are at Lusaka, Ndola, and Livingstone. In addition to private airstrips, there are 12 secondary and 31 minor airports.

Zambia's internal telecommunications facilities are aging but still among the best in sub-Saharan Africa. Close to a million cellular phones are in use, and Internet service is widely available.

TRADE AND FINANCE

With its central position in the region, Zambia is becoming a focus for international trade. The annual International Trade Fair at Ndola, in the Copperbelt, and the Agricultural and Commercial Show in Lusaka attract exhibitors from all over the world.

"Zambia enjoyed the peak of its prosperity in the early 1970s."

—metal analyst Tony Warwick Ching to the BBC's World Business Report

Although Zambia is growing more popular as a lucrative tourist spot for vacationers from abroad, the country's tourism authorities still take measures to ensure that the environment of the resorts is not degraded and that the locals will benefit from, and not be exploited as a result of, the boom in the tourism industry.

Commerce has been facilitated by the liberalization of the Zambian money market. Currency can be changed with very few restrictions, and the illegal money merchants of the past have gone out of business. The banking system extends to all corners of the country, and in addition to local finance houses, banks from Britain, the United States, India, and South Africa operate in Zambia. The Lusaka Stock Exchange was a star performer in Africa within three years of its opening. About 20,000 Zambians have invested in the stock market, compared with less than 1,000 at the opening of the exchange in 1994. Analysts are hoping that the privatization of Zambia Consolidated Copper Mines will spark renewed investor interest in the exchange.

TOURISM

The government is eager to make the tourism sector a substantial source of foreign funds but does not wish to control or dominate the industry. Instead it provides support through the National Tourist Board and participates with the private sector in the Tourism Council. State owned hotels and national park lodges are being privatized and roads to tourist destinations improved. It is not a free-for-all market; Zambian citizens are favored in the issuing of operating licenses.

Unlike South Africa and Mauritius with their beautiful coastlines and beaches, Zambia is not a country for mass tourism. What it wants to see is the development of small-scale but excellent facilities that will enable visitors to enjoy Zambia's unique attractions at close hand.

Tour operators now have the challenge and opportunity to build on and extend the existing facilities. Victoria Falls, undoubtedly one of the wonders of the world, has been Zambia's main attraction for decades, and the South Luangwa National Park is famous for its walking tours

during which visitors can have a close experience of wildlife. Facilities in this park, including lodges and small camps, are well developed, but there is wide scope for expansion here and in the many other parks. Lodges on the shore of Lake Tanganyika offer visitors the opportunity to bask in the beauty of the place and go fishing for the Nile perch and the Goliath tiger fish. Water sports from yachting to waterskiing are popular on Lake Kariba.

Following the journeys of David Livingstone and taking steam locomotive trips from the Railway Museum are among the many excursions that cater to the growing interest in historical tourism. Also of great interest are Zambian festivals, whose color and spectacle, music and dancing draw thousands of spectators every year.

Visitors to a safari lodge are provided with a guide and a vehicle to observe elephants in the South Luangwa National Park.

ENVIRONMENT

THE NATIONAL ENVIRONMENT ACTION PLAN (NEAP) of Zambia identifies five areas of environmental concerns: air pollution, water pollution and sanitation, land degradation, deforestation, and wildlife depletion. The government has come up with plans to implement and enforce internationally accepted standards and practices to improve the quality of human life to meet present and future needs.

POLLUTION IN COPPERBELT TOWNS

Acid rain—a form of air pollution caused by mineral extraction and refinery—has the ability to erode structures and injure crops and forests,

Left: **A village theater group acts out a conservation story in a bid to raise environmental awareness.**

Opposite: **An aerial view of a bend along the Luangwa River shows the mixture of habitats found within Zambia.**

A young girl collects water for her family. Clean water is often located far away for many of the rural people. As a result, youngsters usually forego an education, as the collection of water is given greater priority.

not to mention threaten life in freshwater lakes. Zambia is not spared these destructions. Copper mining is Zambia's economic lifeblood, but decades of copper, cobalt, zinc, and lead mining in the Copperbelt region has left 60,000 children and adults at risk from lead poisoning. In 2007 financiers such as the World Bank and the Nordic Development Fund supported Zambia's effort to clean up waste and resettle people after high lead content was found in blood samples.

WATER POLLUTION AND INADEQUATE SANITATION

Radioactive waste and chemical runoffs leak into Zambia's waters. Victoria Falls—Zambia's only World Heritage Site—is under threat from river pollution as a result of tourism. The locals want resorts and lodges to be built near the falls and along the river banks to provide employment. Conserving the environment is not a huge concern. Environmental activists claim that the Zambezi River, which feeds Victoria Falls, no longer flows its natural course and has suffered a drop in its water level. As a result Victoria Falls is not as forceful as it should be. Overcrowded cruise boats add to the pollution.

The Zambian government has promised to facilitate the supply of clean drinking water nationwide and electricity at lower rates and tariffs to rural areas. Huge amounts of funds are needed to improve water conditions. In 2007 the European Union and Oxfam Great Britain granted Zambia 14.6 billion kwacha (about $3.65 million) to improve water and sanitation services in Western Province. The project will enable 46,000 people in 60 very poor communities to improve their health through access to safe water and basic sanitation and hygiene.

SOIL DEGRADATION

Soil erosion reduces the fertility of land and consequently hurts crop production. Continual use of nitrogenous fertilizer has already reduced the crop yield, resulting in a reduction in the net farm income. Small-scale farmers do not counteract this condition, because of the expense involved.

DEFORESTATION AND WILDLIFE DEPLETION

From 0.5 percent to 2.0 percent of the country's forests are depleted annually through bush fires, agricultural encroachment, and hydroelectric developments. The use of firewood and charcoal adds to the problem. Because forests regulate much of the catchment area of the Zambezi River, deforestation badly affects the water supply, especially during the annual seven-month-long dry season. Efforts in protecting Zambia's land have been successful in some regions. This includes the national forest estate, which makes up 9 percent of the land, including 19 national parks. The country must decide how much of the country should be forest and how much deforestation should be allowed to sustain human well-being.

Zambia's wildlife suffers depletion from small-scale hunting for food by local people and from large commercial poaching operations, especially of antelopes, elephants, rhinoceros, and the large cat population.

An aerial view of the Miombo woodlands in the Luangwa Valley. Lush forests such as these are in danger of being lost as Zambia undergoes industrialization.

55

ZAMBIANS

A COMMON ORIGIN IS CLAIMED by nearly all Zambians. North, south, east, and west, the legends of people who converse in different but related languages speak of a migration from the ancient Lunda-Luba kingdom of the *mwata yamvo* to what is known as Congo today. Some people speak of origins even farther north, while the Ngoni and the Lozi lay claims to a South African heritage. Apart from the more recent immigrants from Europe and Asia, Zambia is a broadly homogenous nation, with few of the ethnic contrasts that characterize Ethiopia and India, for example. Most Zambians regard themselves as the subjects of various traditional rulers, but what Western journalists call tribalism rarely leads to conflict. Zambians remain loyal to their national flag.

Nearly 50 percent of Zambians live in urban areas, where people from different ethnicities contribute to a diverse social mix. The differences in lifestyle that exist are between the rich and the poor, between city sophisticates and their rural brothers and sisters.

The World Health Organization has put the disability-adjusted life expectancy in Zambia at less than 39 years, one of the lowest in the world. This is mostly due to the huge impact of AIDS on the community, with around 17 percent of the population carrying the infection. About 650,000 children have been orphaned due to AIDS.

Left: **Are these people Ngoni, Lozi, Chewa or Lunda? It is impossible to tell the groups apart by appearance alone in Zambian cities.**

Opposite: **A portrait of girl from a Kawaza village.**

Rural women balancing goods above themselves. Though belonging to a tribe may be irrelevant to an increase number of urban Zambians, the majority of Zambians owe some allegiance to a traditional ruler and probably have relatives and economic interests in rural areas.

Most Zambians speak languages that belong to the Bantu language group.

POPULATION

Zambia's population exceeds 11.4 million (2007 estimate), with an annual growth rate of 1.66 percent. Statistics for infant mortality (nearly 101 per 1,000 births, or 10.1 percent) and life expectancy (38.4 years) are unreliable, as many people do not get their births and deaths registered. The country has the highest rate of urbanization in tropical Africa. Internal migration started in earnest with the opening of mines less than a century ago and is continuing, though the government's plan to resettle urban volunteers on rural farms may reverse the trend.

Zambians tend to have large families, both a cause of and a compensation for high child mortality. The Planned Parenthood Association, supported by the government and donor agencies, is active (though opposed by some Christians and Muslims), and there is an ongoing campaign to raise awareness of HIV/AIDS, a disease sweeping fatally through all levels of society.

ETHNIC GROUPS

Most Zambians are black Africans who speak Bantu languages. The colonial authorities, aided by missionaries, divided the inhabitants of Zambia into more than 70 ethnic groups. "Divide and rule" was a convenient policy for the imperial government, which maintained a strict control over the Zambian population through the chiefs it appointed and paid. Where a people did not have a chieftainship, the government created one. To this day a Zambian's reporting tribe and chief are recorded on his national registration card wherever possible.

The major groups in Zambia are loyal to the successors of the precolonial kings. In the west are the Lozi under their *litunga*; in the east are the Chewa (Njanya) under their paramount chief, or *undi*; and the Ngoni, under the *mpezeni*. In the north are the *mwata kazembe*'s Lunda and the *chitimukulu*'s Bemba; in the northwest, the *ishinde*'s Lunda, the Luvale of the *ndungu*, and the Kaonde of the *kapijimpanga*. The

A village chief among his loyal subjects.

Bantu-Botatwe ("Three People") of the south who speak variations of the Tonga language have no paramount chief. Other significant groups are the Mambwe, the Nam-wanga, the Tumbuka, and the Nsenga in the east; the Chokwe and the Luchazi in the northwest; and the Lenje and the Soli in central Zambia.

Urban members of such groups travel long distances to attend traditional ceremonies, and chiefs often tour urban areas to stay in touch with their subjects. By merely looking at them, a person cannot classify the people into different groups as one can in India, where the Sikhs look distinctive from the Assamese. In fact the only distinguishable Zambians are the few unassimilated Batwa pygmies and San, or Bushmen.

Besides tribal, or traditional, loyalty, Zambians classify themselves by clan. Clans are said to have originated during the period of migration

A typical family unit in Zambia.

from the north. A party of migrants would name itself after a significant event, an animal, or a feature of the landscape. Clan names are sometimes used as modern surnames—for example, Ng'andu ("Crocodile"), Mvula ("Rain"), and Chulu ("Anthill"). All clan members, no matter what language they speak or how far apart they live, see themselves as belonging to one family whose members are expected to help each other. A Tonga "Elephant," for instance, is morally obliged to give help to a Kaonde "Elephant." Marriage between members of the same clan is regarded as incestuous and forbidden by custom. The clan system operates over much of Africa.

Clans that were once enemies have over the years transformed their aggression into a game called the joking relationship. This allows for ridiculing and mocking of the most extreme kind until everyone collapses in laughter. A joking relationship exists between the Bemba and the Ngoni, who in the past were often engaged in war. This tradition may explain why Zambians are generally great "talkers" but reluctant fighters.

MINORITIES

There are three conspicuous ethnic minorities in Zambia. People with mixed blood—African-Europeans and African-Asians—are one of them. They are citizens of the country but do not generally owe allegiance to a traditional ruler or belong to a clan. Among them are professionals and the business class, farmers, and skilled workers. During the colonial period they suffered racial discrimination and lived in segregated suburbs.

The second group consists of people who are confusingly referred to as Asians, whose forebears emigrated from India beginning in the 1920s,

Whites are particularly prominent in the agricultural sector in Zambia.

THE ROLE OF TRADITIONAL RULERS

What may be called Zambian royalty does not exercise direct political power. The constitution forbids traditional rulers from contesting in the election to the parliament or local councils unless they first resign their thrones. The constitutional House of Chiefs, whose members are selected by the traditional rulers, is given high status but is little more than an advisory body to which legislation is referred for comment.

However, kings and chiefs are revered by traditionalists as the intermediaries between their subjects and the spirits of their ancestors and, ultimately, God. In the traditional areas, which make up most of Zambia, it is the chief who allocates land and has the authority to withdraw the same. This gives the ruler great day-to-day power. Even under the 1995 Lands Act, a person in the traditional areas may obtain permanent title to land of his or her own only with the chief's consent.

Chieftainship is hereditary, but a chief may occupy his or her throne only after receiving recognition from the president. Apart from their subjects' tribute, chiefs receive a salary from the government, and their palaces are maintained at state expense.

mainly as shopkeepers. Though a minority, they are a strong force in Zambia's business life, owning banks, real estate, and large trading houses as well as being prominent in other professions. Sometimes friction arises between the majority of Zambians and the Asians. Not all of the Asians are citizens of the republic, and the Kaunda government tried to force them out of the retail trade. But the relationship between this group and the majority is mutually beneficial.

Today there are probably fewer than 5,000 permanent white residents in Zambia, and probably no more than 10 percent of them are citizens. There is, however, a considerable transient white population, employed via work permits in business, agriculture, industry, and mining. New legislation allows genuine investors to acquire resident status and to buy land, so the number of whites with a long-term stake in the country is increasing.

SOCIAL STRATIFICATION

In precolonial traditional communities the social structure was hierarchical. The Soli, people living to the east of Lusaka, provide a typical example.

According to Soli historians, there were three classes. The chieftainship was hereditary, with succession through the female line. Only a member of a specific clan, in this case the Beans clan, could become the chief. He or she had a council of advisors, often relatives, and their position was also hereditary. Below the councilors were the hereditary village headmen, who ruled the commoners on behalf of the chief. Chief, councillors, and headmen constituted the ruling class. The villages were usually family units made up of commoners, the middle class. At the bottom of the ladder were the domestic workers, who in the words of historians "provided free labor to the ruling class." These bonded workers were mainly prisoners of war or criminals, but the poor sometimes sold children they could not support into this class.

In modern urban Zambia there is no hereditary ruling class, though one of the reasons Kaunda lost popular support was the suspicion that he wanted to found a presidential dynasty.

Today's elite consists of those with wealth and political power, which enables a person to offer patronage and maintain a following. Except in traditional society, wealth and power count for more than birth.

At the bottom of the social scale are the unskilled workers and the unemployed. But this is not a rigid structure, and the extended family, which is Zambia's basic social unit, may contain members of all classes.

Due to Zambia's population growing faster than its economic development, many Zambians are getting poorer. This translates into a great disparity between the upper classes of society—the university students, for instance—and the majority.

LIFESTYLE

AMONG ZAMBIANS, FAMILY TIES are a powerful force, and the extended family is the keystone of the social structure.

A man normally heads the family, but many Zambian groups are matrilineal—the authority and power to make decisions rests with the mother and her relatives. In traditional society this means that when a husband dies his widow, children, and property are transferred to his mother's sister's eldest son. Today many urban Zambian husbands draft wills, entitling their property to their widows, thus sidestepping the system, but disputes are common, and widows often find themselves stripped of their inheritance by relatives of the dead man. Some Zambian men, including Christians, are polygamous, and it is generally true that in any marriage the wife's position is considered subordinate. These days many educated young women prefer to remain single, even when they have children. But though unmarried, they remain members of the extended family of their husbands.

Broadly speaking, the extended family includes all kin related by blood, all of whom have obligations to each other—the richer helping the poorer, and the aged being cared for. In Zambia it is very unusual and considered disgraceful for the aged to be placed in an old-age home.

Left: **A typical Zambian city house.**

Opposite: **From the harbor, wooden boats and dugout canoes take the local people from Mongu, the capital of Western Province, to their villages along the river.**

BIRTH, CHILDHOOD, INITIATION

Zambia has a high birthrate, and half of the population is below the age of 16. In urban areas, expectant mothers can attend government prenatal clinics, give birth under medical supervision, and receive help and advice from postnatal clinics. Rural areas have fewer facilities, and some of these are provided by mission hospitals. It is not unusual for a woman to have six or more children, though not all survive infancy. In traditional societies, children are treated as young adults as soon as they can perform tasks such as caring for younger siblings and helping about the house and in the fields. These days youngsters start school by the age of six, with many children starting earlier in the cities, where there are numerous preschools run by the government and private individuals.

In traditional families, girls and boys undergo an initiation ceremony on reaching puberty. Girls are taught about sex and the duties of marriage by older women. Depending on their ethnic groups, especially in the rural areas, boys are inducted into manhood by completing feats of endurance. After initiation, the "graduates" are considered ready for marriage. With the spread of Christianity and urban living, these practices are on the decline. However, many adolescents are sexually active, and teenage pregnancy often ruins a girl's education prospects.

Only one-third of Zambian children proceed from primary to secondary education, as there are not enough schools; also, schooling has to be paid for. This, together with general poverty, causes the growing problem of "street kids" in the urban areas.

MARRIAGE

There are two types of marriage in Zambia. Statutory law covers marriages performed by a civic registrar or a licensed priest or pastor. Succession to the widow is provided for, and only the divorce court can dissolve the marriage. Traditional or customary marriage is a contract according to the laws of the community, and the traditional status of the wife and the community's rules of succession prevail. The marriage may be dissolved in a customary court. Both types of marriage are less a contract between two individuals than between two families; marriages are considered an enlargement of the extended family.

Another factor both types of marriage have in common is that the prospective husband is required to pay a bride price known as *lobola* (lorh-borh-lah) to his future wife's family. It represents not the purchase of the bride but a pledge and compensation for lost services; it must be returned if the marriage is dissolved. Traditionally *lobola* was paid in cattle or other livestock, but in urban Zambia payment in cash is common, and the parents of an educated woman may demand a high price. A high bride price may make it impossible for a man to marry the woman who has agreed to become his partner. The weddings of children from wealthy backgrounds are elaborate and expensive affairs.

A wedding procession. Zambian brides-to-be usually attend a bridal shower where they receive advice and gifts from the women-only gathering.

DEATH

Upon a death in a family, as many members as possible visit the home and family of the deceased. Every day at set hours, Zambian radio makes announcements of the recorded deaths, calling on relatives to come together. The deceased's family provides food and drink at the gathering, which may last for several days before the burial. Among Christians, a church service is conducted. After the funeral, the mourners gather at the house. In some traditional societies, the deceased's property is allocated after these rituals, and the relatives decide who is to care for the widow and her children. This tradition is especially beneficial for orphaned children whose parents have succumbed to HIV or AIDS. Unfortunately, under growing Western influence, migration to urban centers is breaking family ties. Extreme conditions of poverty are further eroding these traditional structures, and many orphans are being left with little or no support.

RURAL LIVING

Most land in the rural areas of Zambia is held under customary law. The chief remains the custodian of the land and the person who allocates it for use to his or her subjects. The people living in small villages are mostly farmers; some are traders, and some are government officials. Grain is grown during the rainy season, and pigs, goats, chickens, and sometimes cattle are kept. Cotton and groundnuts are common cash crops, while fishing is an important activity near rivers and lakes.

Many villagers are farmers who live at the subsistence level, producing enough food for themselves and having just a small surplus for sale. Nonetheless they grow 70 percent of Zambia's grain. Poverty characterizes the social scenario in the rural areas. The Kaunda government attempted to improve matters by setting up collective and state farms, but these were a failure. Now laws allow the residents in the chiefs' areas to obtain personal ownership of land, a move the current government hopes will enable farmers to get credit more easily so that they can produce more and become more prosperous.

A typical village consists of thatched brick or lath-and-plaster dwellings, with a meeting place, the *bwalo* (bwah-lorh), at the center. Facilities

A rural dwelling in a Zambian village.

such as schools and health centers may be a long distance away, and the roads are usually poor. During the rainy season some areas can be accessed only by helicopter, and following a season of drought, famine can become a dreaded reality in some places.

By contrast, the commercial farmlands held under private ownership mainly along the railway lines have a much more prosperous air about them. These areas occupy about 5 percent of Zambia's land and are farmed largely by the white farmers, who use modern technology such as irrigation and up-to-date machinery. With irrigation, two or even three crops can be harvested in one year. These farmers enjoy a comfortable if not luxurious lifestyle, and their workers, though often poorly paid, are generally better off than the hoe and ox-plough cultivators of the more remote rural areas.

URBAN LIVING

The cities of Zambia cannot cope with the number of people who inhabit them. While vast tracts of the countryside appear empty of people, the urban areas, where some 38 percent of the population live, are overcrowded and noisy.

Middle-income apartments close to modern amenities—one aspect of urban dwellling.

Shantytowns around the cities may be squalid, but many Zambians see them as the first step into the modern economy.

While a great difference in wealth does not exist among rural villagers, the cities exhibit the extremes—from the Hollywood-style mansions of the very rich to the squalid mud-and-plastic structures of shantytown dwellers. Between these extremes, the majority of urban residents live in small houses in the townships (as the poorer suburbs are called), in apartment blocks, or in dwellings they have built themselves in designated places provided with basic services such as water and sewerage.

Statisticians talk of high- and low-density areas, a euphemism for poor and rich, and it is only the latter who are adequately serviced by the city councils. Residents of some high-density areas within easy walking distance of a city center rely on pit latrines, draw water from polluted wells, and suffer outbreaks of dysentery and even cholera. The Water and Sanitation Association of Zambia (WASAZA) estimates that only 62 percent of the population have access to safe water, while commercial utilities provide water to only 47 percent of the urban population.

The more prosperous areas, even if the roads are potholed, offer much that is available in developed countries—restaurants, five-star

hotels, sparkling supermarkets, video shops. A satellite dish adorns many a suburban garden, along with a swimming pool and a tennis court.

But the cities, uncomfortable and filthy as they may be for the poor, are seen as places of opportunity. The drift into them will continue until the government implements policies that bring prosperity to the rural areas. Zambia faces an enormous challenge not only to lure people back to the country to cultivate the land but also to ensure that city dwellers are provided with profitable employment.

ZAMBIAN WOMEN

Men have traditionally dominated Zambia. The presence of female chiefs and the matriarchal system of succession did little to change the basic division of labor by which women were tied to the household and the fields. A woman's life was dedicated to bearing and rearing children and producing and preparing food. Men did not have to endure this routine. They hunted, fought off enemies, and mined and smelted metals when necessary.

71

A woman gathering corn in the village of Kawaza.

As in many other cultures, in Zambia it is generally accepted that a wife must obey her husband. This is both a traditional and a religious habit. The missionaries started schools for girls, the objective of which was to educate them in a less competitive environment than that of the boys. Today, however, the Ministry of Education insists that there is no gender discrimination in the school syllabus.

Far fewer women than men complete secondary education, but measures are being introduced to correct the imbalance. For example, the government reserves 25 percent of its university grants for women, the remainder being competed for by men and women alike. Education and urbanization are working together to inspire women to carve an identity and make their lives more worthwhile. Issues such as the laws of succession have not been resolved to women's satisfaction, but women may now open bank accounts and obtain credit without permission from a husband or a male guardian.

TRAVELERS AND TRADERS

A woman travels hundreds of miles on the bus from the provincial town nearest her village to sell basket loads of mushrooms in the city. A woman undertakes a return train journey from Lusaka to Dar es Salaam, in Tanzania, more than a thousand miles in each direction, to bring back items to sell that are not available in Zambia. A group of women in the Copperbelt get to know from shopkeepers what goods their customers need and make a round trip by bus to get them in Johannesburg, South Africa. A woman flies to Bangkok and trades Zambian emeralds for the luxuries of Asia. Zambian women's entrepreneurship is unquenchable and overcomes all obstacles, whether it's the arrogance of customs officers (usually male), the complications of value-added tax, or the fluctuating exchange rate of the Zambian currency, in addition to the normal hazards of travel.

Today there are women in all spheres of life—judges, ambassadors, doctors, lawyers, businesspeople. Twenty-two women were elected to parliament in the election of 2006, and women represented 16 percent of the cabinet members. It is acknowledged that women are an important component without which the modern Zambian economy could not operate effectively and progress.

Woman entrepreneurs are found everywhere in Zambia where opportunity presents itself.

SCHOOLS AND STUDENTS

At independence there were only 120 Zambians with university degrees and a mere 1,000 who had completed secondary education. It was around this same time that the mining companies started to recruit Zambians for skilled work.

A priority of the Kaunda government was the rapid extension of educational opportunities. Within a few years of independence, secondary schools were built in all 72 districts of the country. Universal free primary education was introduced, and at the other end of the ladder, the University of Zambia was opened in Lusaka. Technical colleges were expanded or established from scratch, and the University Teaching Hospital was built in Lusaka to train physicians. The Natural Resources Development College set about training students for careers in agriculture, among other disciplines, and the National Institute for Public Administration prepared students for the civil service. Later the Copperbelt University, dealing with technical subjects, opened at Kitwe.

Unfortunately the government could not keep up the initial momentum in this field. By the 1980s much of the education system was in decay. In 1997 only 16 percent of secondary-school graduates who qualified for university could be accommodated. The post-1991 government has established a program to rehabilitate schools, many of which had no desks or even windowpanes. The responsibility of school management was passed from the Ministry of Education to school boards on which parents are

School children in Lusaka. Zambians yearn for education but, though matters are improving, it will be a long time before the nation reaches an acceptable education standard.

The University of Zambia campus in Lusaka.

represented. UNESCO estimated that in 2003, 80 percent of school-age children were enrolled in schools. However, most of them drop out after seven years, when schooling is no longer free. Meanwhile, the University of Zambia and the Copperbelt University have been made autonomous. University and college students often engage in rowdy protests about the level of fees, while schoolteachers are often on strike for better salaries. In response to the inadequacies of the state education system, many privately owned primary and secondary schools as well as professional colleges have been established.

By 2003 up to 87 percent of the female population aged 15 and over could read and write English; the male population lagged by just a few percentage points.

SOCIAL PROBLEMS

HIV/AIDS The first cases of Acquired Immune Deficiency Syndrome (AIDS) were diagnosed in Zambia in the early 1980s, although the disease

A traditional healer operates from a disused van in Lusaka.

is believed to have been present but unrecognized long before that. Today AIDS is moving through the population like a plague, with 17 percent of the adult population infected. As there is no cure for the illness, the Ministry of Health and nongovernmental organizations (NGOs) are campaigning vigorously to persuade people to change their sexual habits, since AIDS is most commonly transmitted during intercourse.

Many economically active people are dying as a result of the disease, while the number of AIDS orphans—close to 650,000—far exceeds even the capacity of the generous extended-family system to absorb. Community programs for the orphans have developed during the past 10 years. The orphans are cared for and attend school. The programs also address their emotional and psychological traumas. Like tuberculosis and syphilis in 19th-century Europe, AIDS is a social disease that can be brought under control only when living standards improve and education makes the population aware of its cause and means of transmission.

CRIME Poverty, rapid urbanization, and the get-rich-quick ethic of crude capitalism have led to burgeoning crime in Zambia during the past few decades. Robbery, car theft, and white-collar crime are commonplace. This is an issue Zambia could deal with itself if the country had not been drawn into the international trade in drugs. During the 1980s Zambia became a transit point for the drug Mandrax, a sedative manufactured mainly in India and with a big market in South Africa. An increasing number of young Zambians are becoming addicts. Under Zambian law, drug trafficking and activities associated with it carry severe penalties. The Drugs Enforcement Commission works to some effect with similar agencies worldwide, but Zambia's problem is only a small part of an international social disorder that seems immune to current methods of treatment.

Billboards and posters are part of the campaign to educate people on the causes of AIDS.

RELIGION

THE PREAMBLE TO the current constitution declares Zambia to be a Christian nation but does not make Christianity the state religion. The rights of adherents of other faiths are guaranteed. The president has appointed a deputy cabinet minister to act as intermediary between the church and the state. Although the majority of Zambians are Christians, many have opposed this provision of the constitution.

There can be no doubt that Christians have made a deep impact on the development of Zambia, as it was the missionaries who introduced Western education. They were also in the forefront of the movement to suppress the slave trade in the 19th century, some of the first mission stations being refuges for liberated slaves. But thereafter missionaries worked hand in hand with the colonial government. Nearly all the leaders of the struggle for independence came out of mission schools. President Levy Mwanawasa, like his predecessors, Kenneth Kaunda and Frederick Chiluba, is a practicing Christian.

The declaration of Zambia as a Christian nation has not impinged on the freedom of other religions.

Left: **A church in a rural village in Zambia.**

Opposite: **Stained-glass windows decorate the Anglican Cathedral in the capital city Lukasa.**

TRADITIONAL RELIGION

When missionaries started work in what is today Zambia, they found they were not preaching to godless people. Although it had no written texts, the traditional religion of people speaking the Bantu languages, who made up much of Africa's population, was and still is a coherent system of belief. The supreme god, who is known as Lesa, among other names, is the creator of the world and everything in it. Mankind was created immortal and only later became subject to death, but human spirits live on, intervening in human affairs and in relations with Lesa. The spirits are, therefore, honored and even worshiped.

Boys of the Mshiki tribe dance during the coming-of-age ritual. This ritual introduces the young adult to the spirits of traditional religions.

The living and the dead form part of a single community, joined together through certain individuals, notably the chiefs, who are also looked upon as priests in some sense, and through mediums, who are believed to be possessed by the spirits. The spirits can be either benign or evil, the latter being the power behind what Westerners call witchcraft, which brings disease, misfortune, and death.

The land remains the foundation of human life in this community. Thus a chief's authority in allocating land has a spiritual as well as a political significance.

Because it is believed that a person's spirit lives on, there is no belief in reincarnation, nor is there a belief in punishment (hell) or reward (heaven) for behavior in the afterlife. People enjoy or suffer their just desserts while on earth, and there is no notion of personal redemption or salvation. Lesa, as supreme god, is present but does not direct human affairs as the Jewish and Christian Jehovah is believed to. In times of trouble or to ward off bad times, people will try to appease the spirits with offerings and sacrifices.

CHRISTIANITY

According to a recent census, in 2000 about 87 percent of the Zambian population was Christian. It is generally agreed that Roman Catholicism has the largest single following. The earliest missionaries in Zambia, however, were Protestants of the reformed churches, represented by the Paris Evangelical Missionary Society and the London Missionary Society, to which David Livingstone, the antecedent of all the missionaries, had belonged. Most of the reformed churches are now amalgamated in the United Church of Zambia. Other established denominations are Anglican, Pentecostal, Presbyterian, Lutheran, Baptist, Seventh-Day Adventist, Jehovah's Witness, and a variety of evangelical denominations. There is also a growing number of charismatic fundamentalist groups that take the Bible as literal truth. Eastern Christianity is represented by the Greek and Coptic Orthodox churches.

A missionary visits a church member.

There are some Africanist sects, which fuse Christianity with traditional religion. A former Roman Catholic archbishop of Lusaka, Reverend Emmanuel Milingo, moved in this direction and practiced spiritual healing. The pope removed him from his archbishopric in Zambia in 1983 for marrying Maria Sung of the sect of the Reverend Sun Myung Moon, called the Family Federation for World Peace and Unification.

Today the most noticeable Africanist church is that of the Zion Apostolics, whose bearded leaders, or prophets, take many wives, like King Solomon of old. A self-sufficient group originating in the suburb of Korsten, outside Port Elizabeth, South Africa, members were at first basket makers but are now also proficient tinkers and metalworkers and

A Roman Catholic congregation at worship. Zambian Christianity is split into many denominations and sects but is known collectively as "the church."

work on communal farms. One of Lusaka's suburbs, Mandevu, which means "Bearded," is named after them. The church has branches all over central and southern Africa.

Of the mainstream churches, the Roman Catholic has gone furthest in Africanizing itself. Colorful ceremonies with drumming, singing, and dancing are part of its Zambian liturgy. This church in particular opposed the one-party state and was instrumental in its downfall, with the bishops openly condemning its corruption and dictatorial practices. But today many regard the Catholic Church's opposition to contraception, including the recommended use of condoms as a precaution against HIV/AIDS, as reactionary.

The fundamentalist groups, to which the president and several cabinet ministers belong, are influenced by the TV evangelism emanating from the United States. These groups hold crusades and demonstrations of faith healing and invite people to be "born again" in Jesus Christ. Their members are known colloquially as born again.

Although various churches disagree on many matters of doctrine and practice, they jointly produce a weekly Christian newspaper, *The National Mirror*, and sometimes work together on social projects. The larger denominations have schools, orphanages, and hospitals of their own, which render valuable services to the country as a whole.

ISLAM AND OTHER FAITHS

Islam was established in the city-states of the east African coast 800 years ago, having been introduced by the Arabs and, some believe, Iranian traders. In the second half of the 19th century, Zanzibar was the principal city of the coast, and merchants from there traveled into the interior of central Africa, taking Islam with them. No large Muslim communities developed in Zambia from this source, perhaps because Islamic Zanzibar was associated with the slave trade, though in Malawi, Zambia's eastern neighbor, many people were converted. Muslims in Zambia are mainly immigrants from the Indian subcontinent and their descendants who have settled along the railroad line from Lusaka to Livingstone, in Chipata and in the rest of Eastern Province.

Mosques are prominent in the main urban centers, and the Muslim community is well known for its charitable work, which includes assistance to Christian hospitals. A newly opened Islamic Foundation near Lusaka offers welfare facilities and schooling to young Zambians, and its activities could lead to an increasing number of converts. Islamic propagation societies are offering free education to impoverished rural populations. Many Christian families have sent their children to Muslim schools in the hope that an Islamic education is better than none.

Zambia's "Asian" community also includes many Hindus. Other faiths include the Sikhs, the Baha'i, and a small number of Buddhists and Jews.

A Hindu temple and a mosque stand side by side in Lusaka.

LANGUAGE

AS INDEPENDENCE APPROACHED, Zambians engaged in a heated debate over the choice of an official language for the postcolonial state.

Pan-Africanists favored Swahili, the main language of Tanzania, Kenya, Uganda, and the Comoro Islands. It is also spoken in parts of Congo, Mozambique, and Somalia, as well as in small areas in Zambia itself. Swahili had the advantage of being closely related to Zambian languages and of not being the tongue of any specific nation or group, having evolved along the African east coast in an interaction between local dialects and Arabic. The pan-Africanist view was that by adopting Swahili, Zambia would be taking an important step toward the goal of African unity and replacing English with a language untainted by colonialism. Those favoring the retention of English argued that it was the most widely used international language. If it had been the tongue of foreign rule, that was now irrelevant.

Left: **A group of men reading a newspaper.**

Opposite: **A woman looks at the local newspapers available at a newsstand.**

Many Zambians are multilingual, and it is not unusual for a conversation to be carried on in several languages, including English, at the same time.

They added that Swahili had, in any case, been the language of Zanzibari slave traders, who had wreaked havoc in the country before the British put a stop to their activities.

As things turned out, English was chosen. Swahili as an alternative has been largely forgotten, to the extent that it is not even taught in schools or universities. The preferred second international language today is French.

OFFICIAL AND SEMIOFFICIAL LANGUAGES

As the official language, English is used in all government offices and by the police and the defense forces. The constitution and all legislation are written and published in English, and hearings in the high court and the magistrates' courts are conducted in English, with translation when necessary by interpreters. The business of the National Assembly is carried out in English, and candidates seeking election must by law show that they can use it proficiently. English is the exclusive language of two of Zambia National Broadcasting Corporation's three radio channels and is almost the exclusive language of television and the press. It is the language of domestic and international business and also the country's lingua franca, enabling people with different mother tongues to communicate.

There are seven local languages that have semiofficial status: Bemba, Kaonde, Lozi, Lunda, Luvale, Nyanja, and Tonga. They are used in the local courts, which deal with litigation under customary or traditional law. They share one radio channel and have about an hour each on television every day.

Bemba, Kaonde, Lunda, Luvale, and Nyanja derived from the ancient Lunda-Luba empire. Tonga was brought by earlier arrivals from the north, while modern Lozi comes from the 19th century Sotho language of the Kololo invaders from the south. The other invaders from the south, the Ngoni, have lost their original Zulu tongue and now speak Nyanja.

THE LANGUAGE FAMILY

The Zambian languages are members of the extensive family of Bantu languages spoken from southern Sudan in the north to South Africa and include tongues as widely used as Swahili, Lingala (in Congo), and Zulu.

Despite the great distances that separate Bantu speakers, their languages have the same sort of grammar and share much vocabulary—in Swahili, Nyanja, and Zulu, for example, kufa *means "to die."*

Foreigners wishing to learn Zambian languages can be frustrated by the lack of comprehensive textbooks, dictionaries, and ordinary reading matter.

The Bantu people are believed to have their roots in eastern Nigeria, and the languages are related to some of those in West Africa.

It is said in Zambia that a Lungu-speaking person from the shore of Lake Tanganyika who walks from village to village for 1,000 miles (1,609 km) to reach Victoria Falls will experience no difficulty with language, as one dialect merges into another along the length of the route. The hiker would cross the Chambeshi River shortly after starting the journey and would end the trip on the banks of the Zambezi. The names of both rivers mean the same, "Big Water": *Cha* and *za* both mean "big," and *mbeshi* and *mbezi* mean "water."

The way Bantu languages work is unique. The system is based on the root of the noun, and nouns fall into different classes, each bearing a prefix that is transferred to the verb and the adjective. To take two short examples: the root *ntu* (in-too) signifies "essence," and the prefix *mu* signifies "living." Thus *muntu* means "person" or "human being." The plural of *mu* is *ba*, so *bantu* means "people." The prefix *i* signifies "inanimate." Thus *intu* means "thing," and *izintu* means "things." A sentence is held together by the prefixes, for example:

Izintu   zonse   zanga   zagwa.
Things   all   mine   are falling down.
The Bantu languages are the most alliterative in the world.

WRITING

Missionaries, who used the Roman alphabet, were the first to put Zambian languages into writing. One of the earliest newspapers in Zambia, the French evangelicals' *Liseli* ("The Pleiades"), was published in Lozi in the early 20th century. Major parts of the Bible have been translated into Zambian languages, though the accuracy of a recent Bemba translation has

A man reads the local newspaper. English is almost the only language of the press in Zambia.

The Alliance Française promotes French with evening classes, libraries, and cultural centers in several cities. Some foreign residents, such as Italians, have schools of their own.

been disputed. In the 1950s the government set up the African Literature Bureau to prepare and publish texts in Zambian languages, laying the basis for nonreligious literary works.

That only seven African languages have been recognized by the government as national and given semiofficial status is in fact a compromise, as there are 73 Bantu languages in use, and some groups feel they have been left out. It is, however, difficult to draw the line between language and dialect, so it is likely the position will not be altered.

ZAMBIAN PROVERBS

Proverbs express succinctly the ethical codes and social relations of the people from whom they spring. Many are relevant to daily behavior, and proverbs from the people as distant from each other as the English and the Bemba are sometimes startlingly similar. The following are from various Zambian groups:

Bemba	• A child who does not travel praises his mother as the best cook.
	• Those who eat iguanas are found close to each other.
Kaonde	• The mouth gets the head into trouble.
	• If you followed what a chicken eats, would you eat the chicken?
Lozi	• One finger cannot crush a louse.
	• A cow does not find its own horns heavy.
Luvale	• Firewood for cooking an elephant is gathered by the elephant itself.
	• The snake bites because its hole is blocked.
Nyanja	• The person who does not listen learns when he is struck by an ax.
	• If you are ugly, know how to dance.
Tonga	• He who asks won't be poisoned by mushrooms.
	• Wisdom can come from even a small anthill.
	• It takes more than one day for an elephant to rot.

(Adapted from *Zambian Proverbs* by Nyambe Sumbwa, published by ZTC Publications and Multimedia Publications, Lusaka, 1993. Copyright reserved.)

LANGUAGE AND EDUCATION

The first years of primary education are given in the semiofficial language predominant in the area: Bemba in Northern Province, for instance, and Nyanja in Eastern Province and Lusaka. Disputes in the past over the boundaries of school language areas were settled by compromise. Beyond these years, English is the medium of instruction, with the Zambian languages studied as subjects. Where resources allow, French is introduced in secondary schools. English is the medium at the University of Zambia and the Copperbelt University. English dominates in Zambian intellectual discourse and has without doubt helped to unite the nation across its linguistic divides, as minor as they may be. On the other hand, it has been realized that Zambian languages must develop if they are to play their rightful role in the national culture.

Children in Zambia are taught in one of the seven semiofficial Zambian languages for a few years in primary schools.

ARTS

THE TRADITIONAL ARTS of Zambia suffered severely during the colonial period. The crafts of the potter and the metalworker were driven almost to extinction by the import of factory-made goods, while music, song, and dance, being associated with rituals and ceremonials, were discouraged and in some instances forbidden by missionaries and the government. The missionaries saw them as manifestations of a pagan culture that should be replaced by Christian civilization. From the colonial government's standpoint, any form of artistic expression that mocked it or reminded people that they had once ruled themselves was a threat to its authority. These arts were trivialized, stripped of their spiritual context, and turned into tourist entertainment.

Similarly, the people's oral tradition—the poetry and stories that formed an unwritten scripture of traditional religion—was ignored by missionaries unless it could be fitted into the Christian pattern of belief.

Soul City, South Africa's premier edutainment project, is an internationally recognized nongovernmental organization. It aims to encourage social and behavioral change through radio, TV, and print. It integrates health and development issues into prime-time television and radio dramas. Soul City began by working with Zambia.

Left: **Wooden craft from Western Province.**

Opposite: **A masked performer from the Luvale tribe.**

A *makishi* dancer. Drama in Zambia has its roots in traditional storytelling, music, and dance.

The Bible, as interpreted by the church, became the source of authority and truth.

The one-party state, which followed colonial rule, also inhibited artistic expression and insisted that it should conform to the party's ideology. But Zambia's artistic spirit has proved irrepressible, and its need for support has led the new government to establish an autonomous arts council funded by parliament. It provides assistance to artists, painters, sculptors, writers, and performers, and these people have made it clear they will not tolerate political interference in the council's activities.

LITERATURE AND DRAMA

Zambian literature and drama have their roots in the storytelling, song, and dance of the traditional village, but there is little surviving record of this in its authentic form. Even in recent decades very few literary works have been published, partly because of the high rates of illiteracy and poverty that restrict the market for books and partly because until 1991 the only publishers in the country were the state-owned Kenneth Kaunda Foundation and Multimedia Zambia, a firm belonging to the churches. Both kept imaginative poets and fiction writers under control.

A few novels in English have been published abroad, notably Dominic Mulaisho's *Tongue of the Dumb* (1971). Fiction in local languages has largely been confined to texts suitable for use in schools. A few biographies, such as Goodwin B. Mwangilwa's *Harry Mwaanga Nkumbula* (1982), and books on Zambian history have appeared.

Drama, on the other hand, has enjoyed a healthy existence. There have been two major influences on the development of theater in

WOMEN IN ART

Women artists face more difficulties than men because the idea of female independence conflicts with traditional values and disrupts the age-old social hierarchy in which women were expected to marry and become housewives. The village division of labor made women responsible for making domestic items such as pots, baskets, and mats, but though these were often works of art in themselves, their manufacture was seen as an element of household life and not as individual expression.

Although women today have as much right to an education in the arts as men, very few have made a mark as painters or sculptors. Men in general can accept a woman working—as a book illustrator, for example—but are opposed to their finding self-realization through artistic creation outside the traditional structures. Husbands find it particularly objectionable for wives to "exhibit" themselves on the stage, and most of Zambia's actresses are single.

Female musicians, singers, and dancers face even stronger opposition and have reacted by forming a pressure group called Women in Music, to strive for the right to follow the career that suits their talents. Women's position in the arts will become more prominent as they thrust themselves out of the constraints imposed by men who act as if the attitudes of the Victorian age in Britain should prevail forever.

Zambia. One is the oral tradition of storytelling, which has led to a widespread preference for what is seen and heard over what has to be read from the page. Another has been the British love of amateur theatricals, which led to the establishment by whites of theater clubs in Lusaka, along the Copperbelt, and elsewhere, often with a proper auditorium and the facilities needed for stage performances. After independence these theaters came under the control of Zambians, and the heritage of the stage play has lived on. The University of Zambia Theater, the Zambia National Theater Arts Association, and others promote theater extensively. Schools, colleges, universities, and even the defense forces have drama groups, while parallel to the growth of established theaters a number of clubs sprang up that rejected the British touch in favor of a postcolonial African approach to drama.

Sensitisation and Education Through Kunda Arts (SEKA) is a collective of artists who create theater to address pressing issues in the community. The group has stated, "We believe in changing circumstances by changing minds through the arts—theater and stories in particular."

Bad Timing, *Zambia's first dramatic narrative feature film, was produced in 2006. It was written by famed Zambian playwright Samuel Kasankha and directed by Zambian Jabbes Mvula, and it starred Zambian actors and actresses. It was shot on location in Lusaka and Livingstone.*

Masks for sale at a craft market in Lusaka.

Plays by Zambian dramatists often deal with social problems (divorce and the laws of inheritance, for example) or historical topics, as in A. S. Masiye's *Lands of Kazembe* (1973). Playwrights and performers are often recruited to tour the country to present didactic plays as part of campaigns against, for example, AIDS.

CRAFTS

Even in the remotest villages, manufactured goods such as enamel saucepans and plastic buckets are replacing traditional craft items. In the urban areas the replacement is almost total. The craft heritage of Zambia's traditional culture is not, however, being allowed to fade away.

In the 1930s the Livingstone Museum was founded with the express objective of collecting and preserving what in those days was called ethnological material. The museum today has as fine a collection as anywhere else in Africa. Since independence, other museums have enlarged the national collection, including the Moto Moto Museum in Mbala in the north, the Nayuma Museum in the west, and the Tonga Museum in the south.

Residents as well as tourists buy Zambian crafts. Interest in African crafts can help to save them from extinction.

The Zambian National Arts Council manages centers where the skills to make the crafts are kept alive. In Lusaka, the Kabwata Cultural Village maintains the resources for men and women to make traditional items for sale. The museums also encourage the production of such objects and buy them for resale. Foreigners—residents in Zambia as well as tourists—buy most of the crafts. This market is also tapped by private entrepreneurs through shops in the major centers. Popular items are baskets, patterned reed mats, carved wooden bowls, baked-clay pots, masks, shields, metalwares, and musical instruments such as drums, hand pianos, and xylophones. There is considerable production of carved and polished wooden animals, birds, and human figurines.

A weaver keeps his art alive in Western Province of Zambia.

A modern urban craft is the making of model bicycles, cars, and aircraft, usually with moving parts, using steel or aluminum wire. Model bicycles have riders whose legs move up and down as if pedaling when the machine is propelled forward. These ingenious and skillfully made toys are often the work of children.

VISUAL ARTS

Traditional baskets, mats, woodcarvings, masks, decorated pottery, jewelry, metal spearheads, combs, and axes were often of great beauty and made with a high degree of skill. But most such works were utilitarian in purpose. The concept of visual art as a means of individual, rather than communal, creative expression is relatively new in Zambia.

Woven baskets for sale at the Kamwala Cultural Center in Lusaka.

Some Christian missionaries, if not the more puritanical churches, wanted devotional woodcarvings and statues as well as paintings for their buildings, and this gave an opening to individual talents. In addition, Western secular education regards art as an essential part of the curriculum.

An art school was established in Lusaka shortly before independence, followed by the Department of Fine Arts at the University of Zambia, where people who chose to be artists or who have a passion for modern arts can receive training. Since then Zambia has produced dozens of fine painters and sculptors, some of them, however, self-taught. Many of these artists' works may be described as social commentary, particularly on the unequal distribution of wealth in the country or the trials of urban life in contrast to the simplicity of the rural past.

THE HENRY TAYALI CENTER

The greatest Zambian artist of the modern period was the painter and sculptor Henry Tayali. Much of Tayali's work depicted the crowdedness of city life and the wish of the soul to transcend it.

The one-party state drew up a policy on the arts intended to bind artists into a "socialist-realist" straitjacket, the kind imposed by Stalin in the Soviet Union, but Zambian artists revolted and founded their own Visual Arts Council (now part of the National Arts Council) to assert their independence. With the help of well-wishers, the council acquired premises for a workshop and gallery in Lusaka, which has become the focus of activity in the visual arts. It is now called the Henry Tayali Center.

Few Zambian visual artists can earn a reliable living from their work alone. While some artists are well known and popular, there are few art galleries in the country that might provide the outlets they need and few private Zambian collectors. Some artists sell their work from door to door; others exhibit in hotels and even private residences. Painters and sculptors who keep up with trends may be fortunate enough to get commissions from banks and other corporations. Despite the difficulties, which include the high cost of materials, Zambia's visual artists are producing an impressive variety of work. Henry Tayali was a famous Zambian painter whose visual art legacy lives on at the Henry Tayali Center, in Lusaka's Show Grounds, which promotes young artists. *Art in Zambia*, a book by Gabriel Ellison published in 2004, is the first to give a comprehensive history of the visual arts in Zambia. Individual talents differ, but the artists' creations are a mirror of the society as well as an expression of the individual genius.

MUSIC AND DANCE

Traditional instruments are still played throughout Zambia, although Western instruments are popular, particularly among the young. The most widely used musical instruments in Zambia are drums, which range in height from 1.5 feet (0.5 m) to 5 feet (1.5 m) and can be as wide as the diameter of the tree trunk from which they were made. Drums in a sequence of sizes form a percussion orchestra to accompany singing

"Like their predecessors in the 1970s who adapted rock and roll to a Zambian flavor and called it Zamrock, our young artists and producers have interpreted the music they have grown up with—R&B, rap, and reggae, for example—and have given it a local twist."

— *Chisha Folotiya, founder of Mondo Music Records*

and dance. Drumming plays an important part of rituals, ceremonies, celebrations, and community interactions.

Another instrument that can be large and impressive is the *silimba* (see-leem-bah), a xylophone-type instrument. The keys are flat wooden strips tied to a wooden frame with gourd resonators, one beneath each key, in a succession of declining sizes from one end to the other. The keys are tuned to either an eight- or a five-note scale, the former close to that which characterizes much Western music, and are struck with a rod topped with a ball of rubber.

The hand piano used to be a popular solo instrument. It features iron keys mounted on a small board, which is sometimes hollowed to form a resonator. The keys are adjustable so that they can be tuned. The hand piano is held between the hands and played with the thumbs. Today the homemade guitar, constructed with a tin can as resonator, is more often heard than the hand piano.

Other traditional instruments include rattles, reed flutes, horns, rasps, and the one-string harp. All the traditional instruments are used and taught at Maramba Cultural Village in Livingstone and accompany the National Dance Troupe, which performs on state occasions and entertains at hotels and concerts.

Traditionally dance formed part of ritual ceremonies, and much of the dancing seen today has been adapted for the general audience.

Traditional singing is in choral form, with a lead voice to which the chorus responds. Solo singing, in the Western sense, is an innovation. Modern Zambian popular music, where the old instruments have given

A drummer performs at a cultural village.

HAIR ART

The earliest European travelers noted with admiration the care with which African women dressed their hair to create stunning coiffures. This tradition has continued, and mothers even today spend hours plaiting their daughters' hair and patterning it in intricate designs. Girls at school spend much free time doing this for each other, and many a young woman goes on to become a professional hairdresser, ambitious to open a salon of her own.

There are innumerable hair salons (sometimes called saloons) in Zambia. Some of them are humble affairs in a thatched hut or under a tree, while others are as up-to-date as anywhere else in the world, with all the equipment and unguents a lady of fashion might require.

A simple style may take only an hour or so to put into effect, but an elaborate creation may take a half-day. Time passes quickly, though, for the salon is not merely a place to have a head of hair turned into a work of art but also a place for the exchange of news and gossip.

way to electric guitars, synthesizers, and factory-made drum sets, is still basically choral as far as the singing is concerned. Individual star performers are rare. Among the young, American and British pop has more following than modern Zambian music. Zambian bands are strongly influenced by Western fashion. A characteristic of the Zambian audience is that it likes its music to be played very loud. Musical tastes reflect the influence of the West and the rest of Africa.

In big towns, nightclubs and shebeens belt the sounds of *kwela* (kwair-lah) and rumba, and many local bands play to the taste of the increasingly westernized youth. Lusaka has its own theater, the Lusaka Playhouse, featuring a variety of local Zambian productions. As part of a shopping complex built near Manda Hill in early 2004, Lusaka has a modern five-screen cinema multiplex, along with a bowling alley and a 200-seat theater that hosts local and regional cultural and musical events.

LEISURE

ZAMBIANS IN THE CITIES have a range of recreational activities to select from, but the choice depends on how much disposable income the person enjoys. Those who cannot afford to join sports clubs or the expensive equipment needed for most Western games are in much the same position as the rural poor, whose choice is very limited. Organized sport is a recent introduction to Zambia, as are facilities and pastimes that depend on electricity, such as the cinema, radio, and television. In traditional life entertainment has to come from the resources of the village itself. Work can be enlivened with singing and dancing, while weddings are often the greatest opportunity to eat, drink, and have a good time.

Local festivals to celebrate the harvest or commemorate the ancestral spirits are enjoyable occasions, but the most regular form of entertainment is storytelling around the fire at night, with a pipe to smoke and beer to lubricate the proceedings.

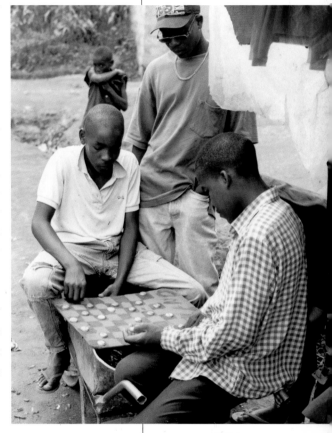

Zambians amuse themselves by playing games like darts, draughts (*above*), and basketball (*opposite*). Many Zambians also love to gamble as a pastime.

POPULAR SPORTS

SOCCER Zambians, rich and poor, urban and rural, are united across all barriers by a passionate interest in soccer (also called football). For anyone who can scrape together enough cash, the radio—used to listen to soccer broadcasts—is as much a household item as a cooking pot.

Soccer is one of the sports in which Zambia excels. The game was brought to the country by the British and was promoted by the mining companies as a recreation for their workers. The earliest teams bore the names of mines, such as Bancroft Blades and Mufulira Blackpool. Over the years other business organizations encouraged the formation of their own soccer clubs, and the sport has now reached the stage where Zambia has a full-fledged professional league. Many players who have become stars in Zambia are taken on by clubs abroad, in Europe, Saudi Arabia, South America, and South Africa. At home the game is governed by the Football Association of Zambia (FAZ) and internationally by the Federation of International Football Associations (FIFA).

It is from this environment that the country's national team is drawn, and that team is among the top three in Africa and among the world's top 20. The fortunes of the national squad are followed with almost religious devotion. Though it has yet to qualify for the World Cup, it has been close to doing so several times since 1974.

Zambian national soccer player Clive Hachilensa (*right*) in action during the African Cup of Nations match.

Zambia has also produced Africa's most famous soccer commentator, Dennis Liwewe, who since the 1970s has been the role model for others in the profession in many countries as a result of his broadcasts on the BBC.

Zambia may be among the best in soccer, but it is a poor country. The football association is always short of money for the development of the game, and the state's contribution to sport as a whole is small. The game extends from its central venue, the Independence Stadium in

SOCCER—DISASTER AND RESURGENCE

The Zambian national team was well placed to get into the finals of the 1994 World Cup and on April 27, 1993, took off from Lusaka in a military aircraft to fly to Dakar for a qualifying match against Senegal. But the team never arrived. Immediately after leaving Libreville, Gabon, after a refueling stop the plane plunged into the sea. Eighteen players, 12 officials, and the entire aircrew perished, and Zambia lost the best soccer team it had ever had, including its captain, Wisdom Chansa.

When the news reached Zambia the next morning, people were so stunned that they shut down their offices, and crowds of mourners were seen weeping in the streets. But Zambian soccer has an inextinguishable spirit of its own, and within weeks a new team had been formed, with Kalusha Bwalya, a Zambian soccer star playing for a Dutch club, as captain.

Against all odds, Bwalya's team came within an ace of qualifying for the 1994 World Cup and winning the African Nations Cup. It was acknowledged to be the best team in Africa. It was as if the genius of the lost team had come back from the dead.

In Zambia donations from the public generated a large sum of money to provide for the families of those who had died in Gabon. The remains of the crash victims were buried adjacent to the Independence Stadium in Lusaka, and a memorial was erected. It has become a place of pilgrimage, and visiting teams go there to pay homage to the dead before their matches in the stadium.

Lusaka, to every corner of the country, and Zambia also has one of the first women's leagues in Africa. Indisputably the national sport, soccer is played even by the barefooted, if only with a ball made of a bag stuffed with straw.

GOLF Another favored national game is golf, but it is confined to the better-off. Like soccer, golf was introduced by the British to the mining towns and the administrative centers. It was for decades a pastime that could be enjoyed only by whites on the many splendid links in the Copperbelt, in Lusaka, and elsewhere.

Zambia has produced not only Africa's best soccer team but also its most famous soccer commentator, Dennis Liwewe.

But shortly before independence it was a Zambian, David Phiri, who became the first African to play golf for Oxford University in England and won the acclaimed status of a Blue, a top sports honor. When he returned home to work for the mines, the "color bar" crumbled. The game was given another boost when it was taken up by President Kaunda. He laid out a nine-hole course in the spacious and elegant grounds of the president's official residence, the State House.

Kaunda is no longer president, and the current president does not play golf, but the presidential links are still maintained and used mainly for prestigious charitable fund-raising tournaments. Zambia, with first-class golf courses in the main population centers, is on the international golfing circuit, and thousands of Zambians play the game regularly. Even small provincial towns have golfing facilities.

BOXING AND OTHER SPORTS Boxing has a large following, too. Zambia has produced three Commonwealth Boxing Council champions—Lottie Mwale (light heavyweight), Chisanda Mutti (cruiserweight), and Joe Sichula (heavyweight). Zambia also has a female boxing champion in Esther Phiri, who took the Women International Boxing Federation super featherweight title in 2007. In other athletics, the hurdler Samuel Matete won a bronze in the 1996 Olympics.

Zambians also swim and play tennis, squash, hockey, rugby, and bowls—a game usually played on grass with large wooden balls. For those with a taste for adventure, whitewater rafting down the Zambezi Gorges below Victoria Falls makes the adrenaline flow, as does stalking big game as a licensed hunter in one of Zambia's game management areas.

David Phiri, the Oxford Blue who ended racial discrimination on Zambia's golf courses.

CHESS International master Amon Simutowe is the strongest chess player south of the African Saharan region. He is currently rated number three on the continent. In the 2007 Euwe Stimulus Tournament, held in Arnhem, the Netherlands, Simutowe earned his third grandmaster. He was the sixth grandmaster from the African continent and the first from the sub-Saharan region.

RELAXING

A favorite way for Zambians to pass the time is, quite simply, conversation. Zambians are sociable people who enjoy storytelling and, let it be said, gossiping accompanied by the consumption of beer. In the village, the traditional meeting place is the *bwalo*. In urban areas, the tavern replaces

Beer has always been a part of Zambia's traditional culture. There is no temperance movement in the country, but a good number of people abstain for moral or religious reasons.

Storytelling under the trees, with ample beer to quench the thirst.

In both urban and rural areas, guitars made of tins and boxes provide hours of inexpensive entertainment for many of the local people.

the *bwalo*. Missionaries and the colonial government tried, with some success, to turn Zambians into teetotalers, or at least to keep "European" liquor out of their reach. For many years the only legal public drinking places in urban areas were so-called beer halls, usually owned by the local council. They were designed along the lines of a village social center, and the only liquor available was traditional beer marketed as Chibuku or Shake-Shake. After independence, beer halls were renamed taverns and continued to flourish.

Bars serve a variety of drinks. The most popular drink is bottled lager. Bars range in quality from cramped shacks in the townships to expensive "pleasure resorts" surrounded by gardens with thatched shelters against sun or rain. There is usually music from a stereo deck and on weekends a live band. People dance and may buy a meal of grilled steak, chicken, or sausages at a barbecue.

For people with money to burn, there are more-expensive pleasure centers in the cities, where they can find everything from casinos with roulette and blackjack to video games to strobe-lighted dance floors.

Cinemas are in the city centers. The wealthy do not go to the cinema at all, preferring to watch a television set tuned to the world via satellite dish or to rent films. Enterprising people in the townships who are fortunate enough to have electricity establish their own minicinemas in their houses with a television set and a video player.

Of all the electronic media, however, radio is the most popular, especially since the advent of the relatively cheap transistor run on batteries. A radio-cassette player can blast out music any time, and it is not unusual in the

WAYALESHI—THE SAUCEPAN RADIO

Radio or wireless, which is known in the vernacular as *wayaleshi* (wah-yair-lair-shee), has held an important place in the life of the country since World War II, when Zambian troops were serving in distant lands. At the time, communications within Zambia were poor, and many of the soldiers' families were unable to read. To keep the soldiers' loved ones informed of the progress of the war and of their men in arms, the government decided to distribute radios to the villages and to the community centers in the towns. But standard radio sets were large, fragile, and expensive, making distribution and upkeep difficult. The problem seemed insoluble until an information officer named Harry Franklin came up with a brilliant idea. In conjunction with the Eveready battery company in England, he designed a simple dry-cell battery set whose valves, circuits, and speaker fitted inside a small, tough saucepan.

The saucepan sets were distributed all over the country, and at the same time Franklin set up Zambia's first broadcasting station in a Nissen hut at the airport in Lusaka. This was the beginning of the Zambia National Broadcasting Corporation (ZNBC), which covers the country with two shortwave channels, two medium-wave channels, and one FM channel. ZNBC also runs public-TV stations that broadcast only from 5 P.M. to midnight and one television channel. Since 1991, three independent radio stations have also come on the air. Zambia's addiction to radio goes back a long time, and the original saucepan radios have become collector's items.

FESTIVALS

ZAMBIANS ENJOY A NUMBER OF annual secular, religious, and traditional festivals and ceremonies. People of all faiths in Zambia celebrate their festivals and holy days free of any restriction.

In the national calendar Independence Day, October 24, is the most important event of the year. In all cities of the republic it is marked with parades, and special sporting events such as the finals of the Independence Cup soccer tournament and the national motor rally take place. Labor Day, May 1, sees parades organized by the trade unions. It has become a tradition for employers to present long-service awards to workers on this day.

The first Monday of August is Farmers' Day, and the Zambia Agricultural and Commercial Show is held in Lusaka over that weekend. The show offers a fine display of Zambia's achievements in the farming sector and is a shop window for industrial products, with many Zambian and

Left: **A May Day parade along the roads of Zambia.**

Opposite: **A performer taking part in a traditional festive dance.**

The royal barge is ready for the annual Kuomboka ceremony.

foreign exhibitors. The show is usually inaugurated by the president or a visiting foreign dignitary, who presents trophies to the prizewinners in categories that range from Best Beef Bull to Best Industrial Stand. The show is also a great occasion for fun, with a military tattoo and other music, equestrian displays, and other entertainment. The Zambia International Trade Fair, held at Ndola in the Copperbelt in July, also offers a weekend of entertainment, apart from the serious business conducted between Zambian businesspeople and the worldwide exhibitors.

The most important festival in Zambia's Christian calendar is Christmas. It is the time for the exchange of greeting cards and gifts, and some churches, such as the Anglican Cathedral in Lusaka, host a charming carol-by-candlelight ceremony. Most industries in Zambia close from Christmas Eve until after New Year's Day, making this a holiday period. Christmas is commercialized in the style of Western consumer societies.

Although not designated public holidays, the Diwali of Hindus and the Eid al-Fitr of Muslims are celebrated by these communities.

TRADITIONAL CEREMONIES

Many Zambian groups hold an annual festival to celebrate their identities and to commemorate the heroes of the past who are now in the spirit world. Some of these ceremonies were suppressed during the colonial period on the grounds that they were heathen, subversive, or both. Under the one-party state the ceremonies were controlled on the pretext that they encouraged "tribalism." Since 1991 many of them have been publicly revived. Some are small, intimate affairs, others large and spectacular. They may be particular to one group but are now regarded as national occasions. Of those, Kuomboka of the Lozi, N'cwala of the Ngoni, Likumbi lya Mize of the Luvale, Mutomboko of the Lunda, and Shimunenga of the Ila are the most outstanding. Zambians of all groups, foreign residents, and tourists are welcome to attend and do so in large numbers.

KUOMBOKA

Kuomboka (koo-orhm-borh-kah) means "to come out of the water" and signifies the greatest public ceremony of the Lozi, the heartland of whose kingdom is the floodplain of the Upper Zambezi. The *litunga* has two capitals, one at Lealui on the plain and another at Limulunga, on rising land on the east bank of the river. The *litunga* and his court split the year between the two palaces. In March or April, when the rainy season has run its course, the plain becomes completely flooded, and Lealui is isolated. The *litunga* must then leave there to go to Limulunga.

At the appropriate time, the royal drums are sounded, preparations are made, and the *litunga* proceeds to the royal barge, the Nalikwanda. Propelled by skilled paddlers wearing scarlet berets, the great barge crosses the floodwaters and docks at Nayuma, the harbor on the shore. Crossing the water, the Nalikwanda is followed by smaller royal barges and a flotilla of canoes.

The music of drums, xylophones, and singers accompanies the *litunga*'s procession, and his subjects wear their traditional Lozi costume, with its brightly colored long skirts. When the *litunga* enters the Nalikwanda at Lealui he is dressed in his traditional robes, but during the journey he changes into a replica of the British admiral of the fleet uniform, which

Paddlers wearing red berets and print skirts move skillfully across the water during the Kuomboka ceremony.

was presented to his ancestor, Lewanika, when he attended the coronation of King Edward VII in London in 1902.

The origins of Kuomboka are hidden in the past, but the ceremony as it now exists, though with a less grand barge, probably began during the reign of Litunga Mulambwa in the 1820s. This was before the English started celebrating Christmas with Christmas trees. Kuomboka can be interpreted as the symbolic annual rebirth of the Lozi kingdom by its passage through water.

The days of the ceremony are a time of feasting for the Lozi and their guests, but the ceremony is not held if the Zambezi fails to flood because of drought.

LIKUMBI LYA MIZE

Mize is the place high up on the Zambezi Plain where the Luvale royal chief, or *ndungu*, has his palace and occupies a throne guarded by statues of lions. Likumbi lya Mize means "the Day (in celebration of) Mize." The festival is held in September, the start of the planting season.

On that day, grounds near the palace become an arena where subordinate Luvale chiefs gather in splendid regalia to await the arrival of the *ndungu*, whose throne has been put in position at the head of the arena. Around the arena traditional Luvale artifacts are exhibited to remind people of their heritage. Baskets, knives, holsters, and other crafts are exhibited, but the pride of place goes to the *lutengo* (loo-tairn-gorh), a working model of an ancient iron smelter, with demonstrations by a blacksmith in the art of making hoes and arrowheads. As the crowd waits, the arena is invaded by *makishi* (ma-kee-shee), dancers wearing elaborate brightly painted masks and tight-fitting costumes woven from different colored fibers. They represent the spirits and act out the history of the Luvale in dance with a thrilling display of gymnastics, accompanied by the insistent beating of drums.

When the time is ripe, the *ndungu*, wearing his crown and ceremonial robes, is carried in the royal hammock from the palace to the throne. The crowd pushes forward to catch a glimpse of him because by tradition he lives in seclusion in the palace. When he is seated, a headman, his body decorated in red and ocher and wearing a headdress of bright feathers, performs the royal dance *kutopoka* (koo-torh-porh-kah). The festival's climax comes as the court bard chants the history of the royal family, urging the spirits to assist the chief and pledging the loyalty of his people.

MUTOMBOKO

Mutomboko (moo-torhm-borh-korh) means "victory dance," and it is also the name of a festival celebrated by the Lunda of the *mwata kazembe*, whose

Two Lunda subjects bow before the *mwata kazembe* during the Mutomboko ceremony.

In the olden days during the Mutomboko ceremony a slave was sacrificed to symbolize the mwata kazembe's victories. Today a goat is sacrificed.

territory lies along the Luapula River in northern Zambia. Approximately three centuries ago the first *mwata kazembe* broke away from the Lunda empire of the *mwata yamvo* and crossed the Luapula River from the west into what is now Zambia, fighting and subordinating the people who stood in his way. The *mwata kazembe*'s capital, the town of Mwansabombwe, lies beside the Ngona River, a tributary of the Luapula. Mutomboko is celebrated here every July 29.

The festival begins in the morning with the *mwata kazembe* visiting shrines and paying homage to the ancestral spirits. Priests smear him with ocher and white sacred dusts, and he proceeds to the banks of the Ngona, where he pours beer and throws food into the waters, saying, "What your fathers died for should follow you." The ritual commemorates the drowning in the Lualaba River in Congo of two of the first *mwata kazembe*'s brothers during the migration.

Members of the royal family, chiefs, and councilors in the Lunda hierarchy wear colorful traditional costumes and take their places in an arena. A huge crowd watching the preliminary dances by girls, selected members of the royal family, and councilors surrounds them. The *mwata kazembe*, clad in his royal finery—modeled on a costume given to his predecessor in the 18th century by a Portuguese ambassador—and wearing his crown, which resembles that of the *mwata yamvo*, is borne on the royal hammock into the arena amid great pomp and rejoicing.

The culmination of the ceremony comes when the *mwata kazembe* rises, to deafening applause, and performs the Mutomboko. He carries an ax and a sword, concluding his dance by pointing the sword to the sky (where he came from) and then to the earth (where his body will rest). He thus unites the spirits and the people in his person. The king, followed by his wildly rejoicing subjects, is then carried back to his palace.

N'CWALA

Formerly suppressed by the colonial government, N'cwala (in-chwah-lah) means "First Fruits and Reinvigoration" and is a festival of the once warlike Ngoni of Eastern Province. The ceremony centers on the ruler, currently Mpezeni IV, whose full title is Nkosi ya Makosi, or King of Kings. In the past the men of the Ngoni, an offshoot of the warrior Zulus of South Africa, were organized in *impi* (eem-pee), or fighting regiments. N'cwala was the occasion for all to gather, be united through the king with the spirits, and be given renewed strength.

The ceremony, with its displays of war dancing, reaches its peak with the slaughter by hand of a black bull, which is then roasted on a spit. The king eats the first piece of cooked meat, and then all the warriors join in, the court bard chanting the praises of the monarch. At the appropriate time, the season's first fruits are presented.

The *mwata kazembe* dances with sword and axe during the Mutomboko festival.

N'cwala is a religious ceremony, and the ritual eating of the bull is symbolically similar to the Christian Eucharist. An Ngoni historian of N'cwala, M. B. Lukhero, comments that the *mpezeni*'s health and strength are identified with the well-being of his subjects and the fruitfulness of nature. His function at N'cwala is to bring back the departed spirits for the good of the people. The Zambian Ngoni are no longer warriors but farmers and cattle ranchers. While in the past the good of the people was achieved by conquest, today it comes from the soil, and the modern-day ceremony is most concerned with food and the prosperity its abundance assures.

Today participants in N'cwala dress in the leopard skins of warriors and dance with spears and shields, ritualizing the past glories. Though the sacred bull is still eaten, so also are the first fruits of crops planted at the beginning of the rains, some four months previously.

SHIMUNENGA

The Ila of Maala in Southern Province, cattle people from the most ancient times, believe their ancestral founder to have been a leader named Shimunenga, who won them their territory by defeating his brother Moomba in battle. Shimunenga, after his death, did not live on as a mere spirit but as a demigod. The Ila's most sacred place is Shimunenga's *isaka* (ee-sah-kah), or holy grove, near the town of Maala. He is commemorated annually in a three-day ceremony between September and November, these pastoral people's New Year season. A direct descendant of Shimunenga, who is considered his guardian and is also a priest, decides the exact date.

The court bard sings the king's praises at the N'cwala ceremony.

The first day of the festival is the women's day. They go around the villages dancing, singing, and drinking. The songs are meant to provoke the men. On this day the men do nothing active except drink beer. On the second day the women pay homage to Shimunenga at his grove. Later everyone gathers at the palace of the chief, or *mungaila*. A sermon is given at Shimunenga's *isaka* on the lives of his people, and speeches are made, followed by singing and dancing until all are exhausted.

On the third day there is an awe-inspiring display of the Ila's best cattle. The herds, led by that of the chief, are driven in succession to singing and the beating of drums. After the roundup the celebration of well-being continues with dancing and games, which include mock battles with real spears and dramatized lion hunts. When it is all over around midday, the people having paid homage and offered thanks to Shimunenga for his beneficence, they retire to drink beer, which is also a libation to the demigod.

Spectators at the Shimunenga festival are warned that to desecrate the sacred grove by entering it can bring dire consequences.

Young participants with painted faces watch the N'cwala festivities.

It is said that a reckless European who ignored the warning not to enter Shimunenga's holy grove died of a sudden illness a few hours after his intrusion.

FOOD

FOOD SECURITY IS one of Zambia's major worries. The severe droughts of 1992 and 2005 brought the country to the brink of starvation, from which it was saved only by swift and efficient government action with food aid and humanitarian assistance from the United Nations and other agencies. Crop failures also contributed to Zambia's famine. Erratic rainfall, with years that recorded less than half of the annual average, and higher temperatures decreased the rate of plant growth, as farmers no longer knew when to plant their crops to coincide with the arrival of rain.

Corn, which was introduced to Africa by the Portuguese centuries ago, has become the staple food for most Zambians. Four other introduced starch crops—cassava, wheat, potatoes, and sweet potatoes—are also important. Before the arrival of these foods, the staple grains were the indigenous millet and sorghum and a little rice. Corn is ground and

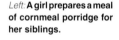

Tilapia is bred in fish farms in many tropical countries in Africa and Asia. The word "tilapia" is derived from tlape *(ti-lah-pair) in Botswana, where Europeans first found the fish.*

Left: **A girl prepares a meal of cornmeal porridge for her siblings.**

Opposite: **Fruits being sold by the roadside.**

cooked with water to make a stiff porridge called *nshima* (in-shee-mah) or *nsima*, which can be eaten with the fingers.

WOMEN AND FOOD

Women grow most of the basic foods in Zambia. In the traditional village, a woman not only spends much time in the fields but also long hours preparing food. She has to collect firewood, carry water from the well or the stream, and turn corn into meal by pounding it in a mortar or grinding it between stones. Cassava has to be soaked in water for a week to remove the poison in it, cut into chips, and dried before it can be made into flour.

Nowadays many villages have a small mechanical mill where grain is ground for a fee. In towns, factory-made meal is available in the shops, and it is even possible to buy precooked *nshima* that is ready to be eaten when boiling water is added to it. In the urban areas, women run most of the food stalls in the markets or on the street. They usually sell *nshima* with grilled steak, chicken, or sausages, though more and more townspeople eat bread from bakeries and fried potato chips. Hamburger with French fries is popular.

After preparing them at home, many a woman will go into the city center to sell a tray of hard-boiled eggs, sausage rolls, deep-fried doughnuts, or roasted peanuts. To a very large extent, it is the women who keep Zambia fed.

ZAMBIAN SPECIALTIES

If carbohydrate *nshima* is the foundation of most Zambian meals, there are many protein foods to go with it. Those who can afford it will have beef, chicken, mutton, or pork cooked in a variety of ways. One way is to grill it over a charcoal fire in a brazier called an *mbaula* (im-bah-ool-lah). Another is in a stew containing onions and tomatoes. Herbs and spices are little used, and Zambian cuisine is generally bland.

Fish is also very popular and comes from Zambia's many rivers, lakes, and wetlands. Fresh fish is transported from its source either packed in ice or in deep-freeze trucks. Much also comes to the markets sun-dried or smoked. The most widely eaten varieties are tilapia, which is raised on fish farms as well as fished, and *kapenta*, the freshwater sardinelike fish from lakes Tanganyika and Kariba.

Other protein foods include field mice, boiled or grilled on skewers such as kebabs, and locusts, several types of grasshopper, tree caterpillars, and termites, all of which are roasted.

Above and opposite: **Corn, a staple food, being pounded into meal and sold on the cob.**

Nshima *can be likened to the Italian polenta. Leftovers can be cut into slices, dipped in egg, and fried in oil to make fritters.*

125

Above and opposite: **A rich variety of vegetables is sold in markets and on the streets.**

The meat of wild animals such as antelope, buffalo, and hippopotamuses has always been part of the Zambian diet, but as hunting is regulated and for some species forbidden, such meat is now less common despite the activities of poachers. Zambia now has a number of game ranches, however, with the result that venison can be found in the shops, but it is expensive. Birds such as guinea fowl, francolins, quail, doves, and pigeons also feed the pot.

Much use is made of vegetables such as cabbages, rapes, and a variety of wild spinach called *libondwe* (lee-borhn-dwair), as well as okras, beans, and fresh or dried peanuts.

During the rainy season, the forests yield a bountiful crop of wild mushrooms, many of which are edible and have a unique flavor. In color they may be white, brown, scarlet, or bright yellow and may look alarming to those who have eaten only cultivated mushrooms bought in a shop. Zambians cook their mushrooms in water or with a little oil. They can be added to meat and vegetable stews, and some varieties are dried for future use. In the rural areas, they are sold along the roadside, though large quantities are brought to urban markets.

Tropical fruit such as mangoes, pineapples, guavas, and wild plums from the forests are eaten daily when they are in season.

Many well-off Zambians have Western foods on their dining tables—cornflakes and bacon and eggs for breakfast, beans on toast as a snack, and roast chicken for dinner—but it would be unusual if *nshima* were not served as part of at least one meal a day.

MARKETS AND SUPERMARKETS

Evidence of how productive the soil of Zambia can be is visible all year round in the markets in urban areas. There are piles of tomatoes, onions, potatoes, cabbages, rapes, eggplants, cucumbers, pumpkins, beans, bananas, oranges, and lemons on offer. Beside the fresh-produce stalls are others selling chickens, eggs, and fresh and dried fish. Visitors from cold climates always express surprise and delight at the freshness of Zambian fruit and vegetables and the full flavor of the meat, though the freshwater fish does not have quite the tang of fish that comes from the sea.

In the brightly lit air-conditioned modern supermarkets, customers find displays of every type of food. There is a butcher's counter with beef, lamb, pork, and perhaps venison, and freezers containing chicken and locally processed bacon, ham, and other meats, as well as Nile perch, *kapenta*, and bream. The dairy chests hold fresh pasteurized milk and cream, Zambian butter, cheeses, yogurt, and ice cream. There are a half-dozen types of bread as well as ready-to-cook snacks such as samosas, spring rolls, and meat pies. In addition, the customer will find a wide range of imported foodstuffs—Greek olives, South African sea fish, Chinese bean sprouts.

A woman ladles out traditional beer.

Chibuku is also called Shake-Shake because the container must be shaken to mix the liquid and the solids.

BEVERAGES

Traditional Zambian beer is brewed from millet, sorghum, or corn. Grain is first malted by being allowed to sprout and then dried. It is pounded into meal and soaked in water to ferment in several stages. The result is a slightly fizzy alcoholic drink. This beer is now also made in factories and called Chibuku.

Some people add sugar to the corn brew to give it higher alcohol content and distill the product using a homemade apparatus of pipes and a cooling bath. The result is a potent spirit called *kachasu* (kah-chah-soo), which is illegal and dangerous to drink. In North-Western Province a strong mead, *mbote* (im-borh-tair), is brewed from honey obtained in abundance from wild bees in the forests.

There is a large market in Zambia for bottled lager, and industrial breweries in Lusaka, Ndola, and Kitwe produce several brands of varying strengths. Wine is made on a small scale from grapes and other fruit. A firm in Lusaka manufactures various brands of brandy, gin, whisky, and vodka, but these products do not compare in quality with those imported from South Africa or Europe.

Tea and coffee are not widely consumed, though Zambia produces tea and a fine arabica coffee, which is much in demand abroad, especially in Germany. The most popular nonalcoholic drinks are carbonated products such as Coca-Cola, Pepsi, Sprite, and Fanta.

DINING OUT IN LUSAKA

Lusaka, the capital and business center of Zambia, has a large diplomatic corps and many tourists passing through. Many restaurants of international standard cater to them as well as to the local clientele, and typically for this part of Africa, many of them are steak houses where Zambian beef is grilled to perfection. In addition, Chinese, Indian, Pakistani, Lebanese, Greek, and Italian cuisines can be savored, while the large hotels regularly feature the Zambian menu.

TRADITIONS AND ETIQUETTE

It is not customary for Zambians to invite guests to their homes. Westerners may find this disconcerting and see it as a sign of unfriendliness. But that is not the case at all. Zambians expect friendly acquaintances to call on them unannounced.

They will be treated as honored guests and immediately offered a drink and a snack. If mealtime is approaching the visitor will be asked to join in. It is customary to cook more food than needed for the family, just in case visitors should arrive.

A favorite traditional nonalcoholic drink is munkoyo, *a sweet beerlike drink named after a tuber that is its main ingredient.*

ZAMBIAN FRESH MEAT STEW

1 pound (450 g) beef, lamb, or chicken, cut into cubes
2 cups (500 ml) water
3 onions, sliced
1 tomato, peeled and sliced
1/4 to 1/2 cup (60–120 ml) peanut oil
2 chili peppers or 1/2 to 1 tablespoon (5–10 g) crushed red pepper

In a heavy stewing pan combine meat, water, and onions. Bring the mixture to a boil and simmer for 30 minutes. Add the tomato slices, oil, and chili peppers. Continue to simmer for about 30 to 45 minutes till the meat is tender. This recipe makes four to six servings. Eliminate the pepper for a southern Zambian version. In Zambia, this dish would be served with *nshima*. This recipe makes two servings.

SWEET POTATO PUDDING

1 pound (450 g) sweet potatoes
1 egg
1–1½ (240–360 ml) cup milk
3 tablespoons (25 g) grated coconut
1/2 cup (100 g) sugar
2 tablespoons (15 g) baking powder
Butter for greasing dish

Preheat the oven to 350° F (180° C). Boil the sweet potatoes till they turn soft. Peel and mash the cooked sweet potatoes. Beat the egg slightly. Mix the mashed sweet potatoes and remaining ingredients. Pour contents into a greased dish, and bake in the oven until the top of the pudding browns nicely. This recipe makes four servings.

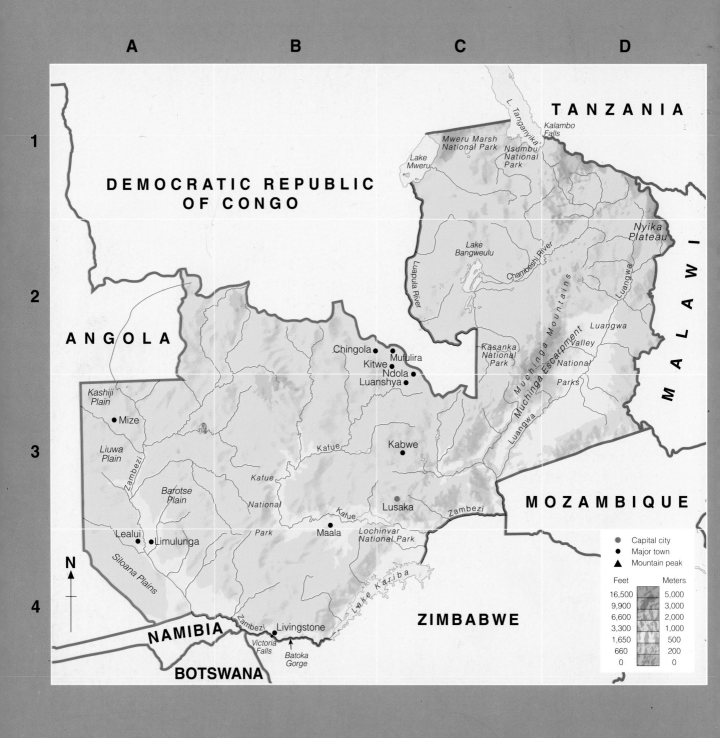

A B C D

1

DEMOCRATIC REPUBLIC
OF CONGO

TANZANIA

L. Tanganyika

Kalambo
Falls

Mweru Marsh
National Park

Nsumbu
National
Park

Lake
Mweru

Nyika
Plateau

Lake
Bangweulu

Chambeshi River

Muchinga Mountains

Luangwa

ANGOLA

2

Luapula River

Kasanka
National
Park

Luangwa
Valley

M A L A W I

Chingola
Mufulira
Kitwe
Ndola
Luanshya

National

Parks

Muchinga Escarpment

Luangwa

Kashiji
Plain

Mize

Liuwa
Plain

Kafue

Kabwe

3

Kafue

Zambezi

Barotse
Plain

Kafue

National

Lusaka

Zambezi

MOZAMBIQUE

Lealui
Limulunga

Park

Kafue

Maala

Lochinvar
National
Park

Siloana Plains

N

Lake Kariba

4

Zambezi

Livingstone

ZIMBABWE

NAMIBIA

Victoria
Falls

Batoka
Gorge

BOTSWANA

Feet	Meters
16,500	5,000
9,900	3,000
6,600	2,000
3,300	1,000
1,650	500
660	200
0	0

● Capital city
● Major town
▲ Mountain peak

MAP OF ZAMBIA

ECONOMIC ZAMBIA

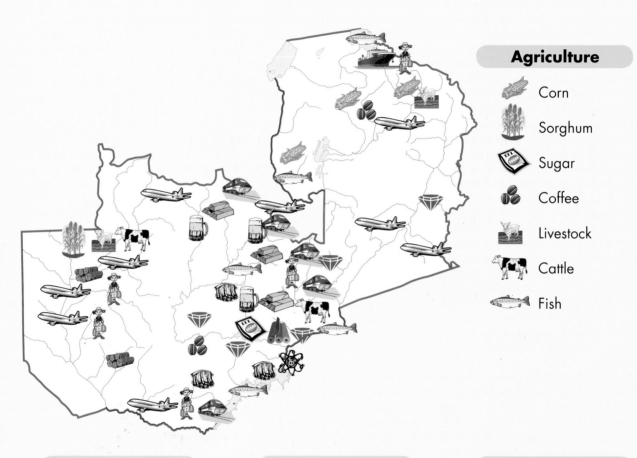

Agriculture

- Corn
- Sorghum
- Sugar
- Coffee
- Livestock
- Cattle
- Fish

Manufacturing

- Textile
- Beer

Natural Resources

- Copper and cobalt
- Gemstones
- Gold
- Hydropower
- Uranium
- Timber

Services

- Airport
- Port
- Tourism
- Train station

ABOUT
THE ECONOMY

OVERVIEW
Progress in privatization and budgetary reform failed to reduce poverty significantly. The country needs an economic growth of 7 percent to support the rapid population growth and to reduce poverty brought about by HIV/AIDS-related issues. Significant debt relief and cancellation of outstanding debt from the International Monetary Fund (IMF) and the World Bank reduced the strain already placed on the government. Zambia is pursuing an economic diversification program to reduce the economy's reliance on the copper industry. By promoting its rich resources in agriculture, tourism, gemstone mining, and hydropower, Zambia may see better days ahead.

GROSS DOMESTIC PRODUCT (GDP)
$15.93 billion (2007 estimate)

GDP GROWTH
5.3 percent (2007 estimate)

GDP PER CAPITA
$1,400 (2007 estimate)

GDP BY SECTOR
Agriculture, 17.6; percent industry, 26 percent; services, 56.5 percent (2007 estimates)

INFLATION RATE
10.5 percent (2007 estimate)

CURRENCY
Zambian kwacha (ZMK)
Notes: 10, 20, 50, 100, 500, 1,000 kwacha
1 USD = 3,735.5 ZMK (November 2007)

LAND USE
Arable land, 6.99 percent; permanent crops, 0.04 percent; other, 92.97 percent (2005 estimates)

NATURAL RESOURCES
Copper, cobalt, zinc, lead, coal, emeralds, gold, silver, uranium, and hydropower

AGRICULTURAL PRODUCTS
Corn, sorghum, rice, peanuts, sunflower seeds, vegetables, flowers, tobacco, cotton, sugarcane, cassava (tapioca), coffee, cattle, goats, pigs, milk, eggs, and hides

INDUSTRIES
Copper mining and processing, construction, foodstuffs, beverages, chemicals, textiles, and horticulture

MAJOR EXPORTS
Copper, cobalt, electricity, tobacco, flowers, and cotton

MAJOR IMPORTS
Machinery, transportation equipment, petroleum products, electricity, fertilizer, foodstuffs, and clothing

MAIN TRADE PARTNERS
South Africa, Switzerland, United Kingdom, Zimbabwe, Democratic Republic of Congo, and Tanzania

POPULATION BELOW POVERTY LINE
86 percent (1993 estimate)

WORKFORCE
4.99 million (2007 estimate)

UNEMPLOYMENT RATE
50 percent (2000 estimate)

EXTERNAL DEBT
$2.798 billion (2007 estimate)

CULTURAL ZAMBIA

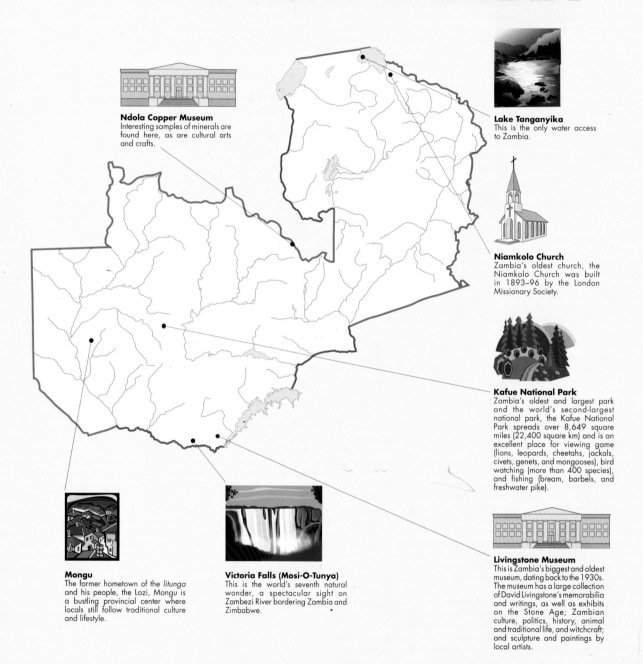

Ndola Copper Museum
Interesting samples of minerals are found here, as are cultural arts and crafts.

Lake Tanganyika
This is the only water access to Zambia.

Niamkolo Church
Zambia's oldest church, the Niamkolo Church was built in 1893–96 by the London Missionary Society.

Kafue National Park
Zambia's oldest and largest park and the world's second-largest national park, the Kafue National Park spreads over 8,649 square miles (22,400 square km) and is an excellent place for viewing game (lions, leopards, cheetahs, jackals, civets, genets, and mongooses), bird watching (more than 400 species), and fishing (bream, barbels, and freshwater pike).

Livingstone Museum
This is Zambia's biggest and oldest museum, dating back to the 1930s. The museum has a large collection of David Livingstone's memorabilia and writings, as well as exhibits on the Stone Age; Zambian culture, politics, history, animal and traditional life, and witchcraft; and sculpture and paintings by local artists.

Mongu
The former hometown of the *litunga* and his people, the Lozi, Mongu is a bustling provincial center where locals still follow traditional culture and lifestyle.

Victoria Falls (Mosi-O-Tunya)
This is the world's seventh natural wonder, a spectacular sight on Zambezi River bordering Zambia and Zimbabwe.

ABOUT THE CULTURE

OFFICIAL NAME
Republic of Zambia

FLAG DESCRIPTION
A green backdrop with an orange soaring eagle at the upper right corner above a panel of three vertical bands of red, black, and orange. Green represents agriculture and other natural resources; red, the struggle for freedom; black, the people of Zambia; and orange, the country's natural resources and mineral wealth. The eagle in flight symbolizes the people's ability to soar above the nation's problems.

NATIONAL ANTHEM
"Stand and Sing of Zambia, Proud and Free." Words were written collectively and adopted by the republic in 1961. Music by Mankayi Enouch Sontmga (1904).

CAPITAL
Lusaka

POPULATION
Nearly 11.5 million (2007 estimate).

BIRTHRATE
40.78 births per 1,000 Zambians (2007 estimate)

AGE DISTRIBUTION
0–14 years: 45.7 percent; 15–64 years: 51.9 percent; 65 years and over: 2.4 percent (2007 estimates)

DEATH RATE
21.46 deaths per 1,000 Zambians (2007 estimate)

INFANT MORTALITY RATE
100.71 deaths per 1,000 Zambians (2007 estimate)

LIFE EXPECTANCY
38.4 years (2007 estimate)

ETHNIC GROUPS
African, 98.7 percent; European, 1.1 percent; other, 0.2 percent (2007 estimates)

RELIGIOUS GROUPS
Christian, 50–75 percent; Muslim and Hindu, 24–49 percent; indigenous beliefs, 1 percent

MAIN LANGUAGES
English (official) and about 70 indigenous languages. Major vernaculars: Bemba, Kaonda, Lorzi, Lunda, Luvale, Nyanja, and Tonga.

LITERACY RATE
80.6 percent (2003 estimate)

IMPORTANT HOLIDAYS
New Year's Day (January 1); Good Friday to Easter (March/April); Africa Freedom Day (May 29); Independence Day (October 24); Christmas Day (December 25)

POLITICAL LEADERS
Kenneth Kaunda (1964–91)
Frederick Chiluba (1991–2001)
Levy Mwanawasa (2002–)

TIME LINE

IN ZAMBIA	IN THE WORLD
1600–1800 A.D. Original San inhabitants pushed out by migrating Bantu-speaking people from the north.	**1620 A.D.** Pilgrims sail the *Mayflower* from England to America.
1851 British missionary Dr. David Livingstone's first visit	**1869** The Suez Canal is opened.
1889 Britain establishes control over Northern Rhodesia using a system of indirect rule, which leaves power in the hands of local rulers.	
1909 The central railroad from Livingstone to Ndola is completed. About 1,500 Europeans are settled in the country.	**1914** World War I begins.
Late 1920s Discovery of extensive copper deposits leads to extension of railway and the building of smelting plants in the Copperbelt.	
1935 Colonial government makes Lusaka capital of Northern Rhodesia.	
1939 Zambia becomes a major producer of copper, drawing European technicians and administrators, who become a dominant influence on Zambian life.	**1939** World War II begins. **1945** The United States drops atomic bombs on Hiroshima and Nagasaki. **1949** NATO is formed.
1953–63 Northern Rhodesian, Southern Rhodesia and Nyasaland are a federation	
1964 On October 24, Zambia gains independence from Britain, with Kenneth Kaunda as the first elected president.	**1966–69** The Chinese Cultural Revolution

IN ZAMBIA	IN THE WORLD
1967	
The Currency Act replaces the pound/shilling currency with decimalized kwacha notes and ngwee coins.	
1972	
Zambia becomes a one-party state, with UNIP as the only legal political party.	**1975**
	Khmer Rouge occupies Cambodia, led by Pol Pot.
1980s and 1990s	
Declining copper prices and prolonged drought hurt the economy.	**1986**
	Nuclear power disaster at Chernobyl in Ukraine
1991	**1991**
President Kaunda voted out of office. Multi-party constitution adopted. Movement for Multiparty Democracy (MMD) wins, and Frederick Chiluba is elected president.	Breakup of the Soviet Union
1992	
Great drought	
1996	
Constitution changed (to bar Kaunda from future election). President Chiluba is reelected.	**1997**
	Hong Kong is returned to China.
1998	**1998**
Celtel begins phone operations in Zambia.	Pol Pot dies.
2000	
Severe droughts lead to severe food shortages.	
2001-2002	**2001**
Levy Mwanawasa is elected president. Zambia appeals for aid after poor harvests caused by floods and droughts. President Mwanawasa declares a national food crisis, with 4 million people facing starvation due to drought. Zambian government rejects donations of genetically modified corn from United States.	Terrorists crash planes in New York, Washington DC, and Pennsylvania.
	2003
	War in Iraq begins.
2005	
Reports say that at least 1 million Zambians are HIV infected and 1–2 percent of population has AIDS.	
2006	
Government moves toward market-oriented economy. President Mwanawasa is reelected for a second term.	

GLOSSARY

Bantu
"People," also used to describe an African tribe and language

Batwa
"Small people"—that is, pygmies

bwalo (bwah-lorh)
Village meeting place

Chibuku
Factory-made traditional beer

kachasu (kah-chah-soo)
Illicit distilled alcohol

kapenta (kah-paint-ah)
Sardinelike fish

kufa (koo-fah)
Word for "to die" in several Bantu languages

Kuomboka
Lozi ceremony; literally "to come out of the water"

kwacha
Zambian currency

Lesa
In indigenous religion, the supreme creator

Liseli
Earliest newspaper in Zambia, published in Lozi in the early 20th century

libondwe (lee-borhn-dwair)
Wild spinach

lobola (lorh-borh-lah)
Bride price

makishi (ma-kee-shee)
Dancers at the Likumbi lya Mize festival

Mandevu
Literally, "bearded"; refers to the Zion Apostolics

mbote (im-borh-tair)
Honey beer or mead

mbaula (im-bah-ool-lah)
Charcoal grill.

Mosi-O-Tunya
Zambian name for Victoria Falls

munkoyo (moon-korh-yorh)
Wild tuber used in making sweet beer.

Mutomboko *(moo-torhm-borh-korh)*
Victory dance festival of the Lunda

N'cwala *(in-chwah-lah)*
First Fruits and Reinvigoration festival of the Ngoni

nshima (in-shee-mah)
Thick corn porridge

nsolo (in-sorh-lorh)
Traditional game played with counters and two or more rows of holes on a board or on the ground

shimunenga *(shee-moo-nairn-gah)*
Ancestral founder of the Ila of Maala

*tlape (ti*ᛁ*lah-pair)*
Word for "African tilapia"

wayaleshi (wah-yair-lair-shee)
Wireless; radio set

FURTHER INFORMATION

BOOKS

McIntyre, Chris. *Zambia: The Bradt Travel Guide*. Guilford, CT: The Globe Pequot Press, 2004.
Taylor, Scott D. *Culture and Customs of Zambia*. Westport, CT: Greenwood Press, 2006.
Musambachime, Mwelwa. *Basic Facts on Zambia*. Bloomington, IN: AuthorHouse, 2005.

WEB SITES

BBC News Country Profile: Zambia.
    http://news.bbc.co.uk/1/hi/world/africa/country_profiles/1069294.stm
Central Intelligence Agency World Factbook (select Zambia from the country list). www.cia.gov/cia/
    publications/factbook/index.html
Copperbelt Environment Project. www.cepzambia.org.zm
Mining in Zambia—Investment Opportunities. www.zambiamining.co.zm
The New Deal Administration's Vision. www.statehouse.gov.zm
The Zambian. www.thezambian.com

MUSIC

Mondo Music Corporation. www.mondomusic.co.zm
Zambush. http://worldmusic.nationalgeographic.com/worldmusic

BIBLIOGRAPHY

BOOKS

Chan, Stephen, *Kaunda and Southern Africa*. London: I. B. Tauris, 1991.

Hamalenga, Munyonzwe. *Class Struggle in Zambia and the Fall of Kenneth Kaunda*. Lanham, MD: University Press of America, 1992.

Johnson, Walton R. *Worship and Freedom: A Black American Church in Zambia*. Ann Arbor, MI: Books on Demand, 1977.

Livingstone, David. *Letters and Documents: The Zambian Collection*, ed. T. Holmes. Bloomington, IN: Indiana University Press, 1990.

Prins, Gwyn. *The Hidden Hippopotamus*. New York: Cambridge University Press, 1980.

Roberts, Andrew. *A History of Zambia*. New York: Holmes & Meier Publishers, 1976.

Ter Haar, Gerrie. *Spirit of Africa: The Healing Ministry of Archbishop Milingo of Zambia*. Lawrenceville, NJ: Africa World Press, 1992.

Vaughn, Richard and Murphy, Ian (illustrator). *Zambia*. New York: CBC Publishing, 1992.

WEB SITES

Central Intelligence Agency World Factbook (select Zambia from country list) www.cia.gov/cia/publications/factbook/index.html

The Official SADC Trade, Industry, and Investment Review 2006. www.sadcreview.com

Southern African Regional Poverty Network. www.sarpn.org.za

U.S. Department of State. www.state.gov/p/af/ci/za

Zambian Government. www.statehouse.gov.zm

The Zambian National Tourist Board. www.zambiantourism.com

INDEX

143